D0857459

Praise for All 37 Days

A perfect time.

Extreme Thought Makeover™ came to me at a perfect time in my life. I was in a rut of everyday routine so the lessons and exercises were a great way to bring awareness of where my thinking was out of balance. The lessons gave new ideas to follow that *worked* and added a new, positive outlook to the ones I was already practicing. Positive images, self-love, gratitude, detachment, giving, pay your bills forward, all meant so much. Your book is awesome.

— *Jolly Stickley, Staunton, Virginia, author of* Energy Restructure: Set Yourself Free Using 9 Layers of the Emotional Body

Help in a profound way.

Rick reveals the information that you are looking for to help you know what to do to clear the blocks that are standing in the way of your most joyful, free life. He is clear and direct and can help you in a profound way, in a very short period of time.

— *Shannon Carney, Squeeze Studio Fitness, Brookfield, Wisconsin*

Choosing the better thought.

It all comes down to choosing the better thought. I've been trying to do this for years! Some days it is easy and, as in life, some days not so much. All the material I choose to read is on a positive note ... I love yours and look forward to reading something from you each day ... that is key. You are doing a great service and I thank you!

— *Jenifer Berg, Beverly Hills, Michigan*

We are making it required training for our dealers.

I have spent over $100,000 on personal development, and this program is my favorite. This is making a really big difference for us. I am going to make this program required success training for all of our new dealers.

— *Bill Driscoll, VP of Training and Dealer Development, DeTech Firesense Technologies, Saukville, Wisconsin*

My clients can do this at home.

After 20 years as a Life Coach, I didn't think I could get this excited about a new program. It's a whole new genre in learning. I have been hoping and looking for something like this that my clients can do at home to shift their consciousness.

— *Sunni Boehme, Life Coach, Bay View, Wisconsin*

We can have it all.

What is between our own ears is our biggest block to achieving our goals. This program has shown us that with simple thought and the power of love, we can have it all.

— *Dr. James Haakenson, Owner, Rhythm of Life Chiropractic, Oconomowoc, Wisconsin*

Starting every day out right.

I am really enjoying the Extreme Thought Makeover™. It really helps me start my day out right and with intention. I enjoy that each daily lesson/exercise is concise and not very time consuming, yet it directs my entire day! Talk about the power of fifteen minutes!

— *Melissa Malueg, Life-Success Consultant, CEO of Xtreme Results, Raleigh, North Carolina*

A great place for people to start.

Thanks for sharing this makeover. I think it could be exceptional for taking people from "less than" space to a fuller, deeper connection with themselves and others.

— *Susan Fox, Rockford, Illinois*

The program is great.

The program is great! I have found myself reading it over breakfast each morning. I've implemented many of these things, especially the bathroom university.

— *Suzanne Monroe, www.iawp-connect.com, Founder & CEO, The International Association of Wellness Professionals*

You have supported me.

I thank you from the depths of my heart for providing this tour through 37 lessons of Extreme Thoughts. It has supported me in mak-

ing my biggest mental advance, in the letting go of old stuff and helping me in looking inside and discovering a magnificent, powerful soul who only wants to love and spread love. Fill your own tank first, your motto for Day 25, has been the most meaningful lesson for me while changing most of my priorities and having the most loving returns. Eternal thanks.
— *Rita Kirschner, Spain*

I'm becoming more optimistic in all the areas of my life.
Everything in the 37 Days has been helpful to me because I'm becoming more optimistic in all the areas of my life. I believe my health continues to benefit from it. Once again, many thanks for the opportunity to take part in your 37 Day Extreme Thought Makeover™ course.
— *Gemma Ward, New Zealand*

Dr. Rick gives hope ... and once you have that you have everything.
I met Dr. Rick Schaefer, who always talked about being positive every moment of life. After the program, I was more than hopeful; I could see and feel the success coming back to me. Dr. Rick's program is all about taking steps that bring inner shifts, and with them, hope. Once you have that, you have everything.
— *Sonny Ahuja, Grand Perfumes, Milwaukee, Wisconsin*

It is beginning to change my life in ways I couldn't have imagined.
It is beginning to change my life in ways I couldn't have imagined. I am so grateful for this wonderful information. I have a long way to go and it is a lifetime journey. This program has been such a positive guide on my journey and at the perfect time.
— *Janet Boyd, United Kingdom*

I can't thank you enough.
It's been quite the eye opener and a very new process doing my daily meditations in the light of what I really want, not what I think I should be doing. I had no idea how much this is new to me, to act upon who I really am and wish to be. I can't thank you enough for the inspiration, and for bringing this program to this world.
— *Sabine Theissen, Toronto, Canada*

Negative thoughts are a distant memory.

The ETM program has had a huge impact on my life. The lesson on Appreciation is something that I try to focus on every day. It is so easy to get caught up in worry, fear and other negative thoughts. When any of these thoughts creep into my consciousness, I focus instead on one small thing that I appreciate. This one thought then leads to others and before you know it, the negative thoughts are a distant memory.

— *Dr. Chris Milkie, Mayfair Foot Clinic, Wauwatosa, Wisconsin*

Thank you!

Thank you so much! Your program has helped me a lot, especially in this very challenging time. Most rewarding and the most enjoyable part of the program is Day 2 when I go back and count my blessings ... It's countless! I never thought life could be so beautiful even amidst struggles, trials and challenges! It made me feel good almost instantly. This is *real help* ... something that I can actually *do* whenever I need a boost. Thank you. Ciao!

— *Ana, Olongapo City, Zambales, Philippines*

extreme thought MAKEOVER™

... 37 Days To Maximum Life!

extreme thought MAKEOVER™

... 37 Days To Maximum Life!

Rick Schaefer, M.D.

Realityls Books

For more information, contact Dr. Rick Schaefer at 414-573-8880.
Mailing address:
Rick Schaefer, M.D.
Extreme Thought Makeover™, LLC
P.O. Box 5333
Elm Grove, WI 53122
http://www.rickschaefermd.com

First American Hardcover Edition
First printing 2010

ISBN-13/EAN: 978-0-9843883-0-1
Library of Congress Control Number: 2010931825

Dedication

To me! Because the only path to truly loving others and living a full and joyful life is in finding complete acceptance and love for the self. I thank all of you who have contributed to my journey toward this end.

And to my mother, Elnora Theresa Schaefer, who brought me the greatest wisdom of my life: advice to "Follow your heart."

Table of Contents

Foreword

Research is summarized by Malcolm Gladwell in his book *Outliers* wherein he mentions numerous times what he titles the "10,000-Hour Rule"—claiming that the key to success in any field is, to a large extent, a matter of practicing a specific task for a total of around 10,000 hours. He describes the 10,000 hours Bill Gates worked in his field prior to exploding into our lives, as well as personages like Wayne Gretzky, Madame Curie, Mozart, Robert Oppenheimer, and the Beatles! Following on the heels of *The Tipping Point,* his first book published in 2000, *Outliers* debuted at #1 on the *New York Times* bestseller list! Gladwell had received a $1.5 million advance on his first book and, trust me, you do not pull down that kind of cash or shoot to the top of the bestseller list unless you are onto something.

I woke up at 28! At that moment, it was very obvious that I had been sleepwalking my whole life up to that point. Unfortunately for you, that means you are reading a foreword by a guy who took over 10,000 *days* to wake up—not 10,000 hours. I had been very good at appearing to be awake for 28 years, but then, boom. And I mean *boom!* I woke up. I discovered how powerful thoughts were. Nothing was ever the same.

Fortunately for you, Dr. Rick (he is an M.D.) woke up a lot sooner and has decided to take some of his awake time and write this guide for you. Nobody pays you to develop a program. No one supports you, or even gives a good goldurn while you are doing it. And, as you will learn, Rick is super smart. He knows there are many ways to get rich and none of them include writing a self-help book. Years of Rick's time went into the research and development of the Extreme Thought Makeover™ program—all of which had to happen before he wrote the first line!

Now, ask yourself, "Why would he do that?" I think it important to know an author's motivations when you are about to invite him into your life. Self-help is about as intimate as you can get. If not, it simply does not work. The reason Rick wrote this book is because he cares. Rick saw so much great potential not being realized. He watched people with such great promise, talent, abilities, intelligence, and compassion going right down the toilet and couldn't stand it any longer. If nothing can be done, then tsk, tsk—make peace with it, but when you *know* something can be done, only the cold-hearted can look the other way.

I once knew an old auctioneer who would hold up a rare item and say, "Folks, you have to *find* one of these before you can buy it. Well, the finding's been done fer ya." Once you finish *Extreme Thought Makeover™... 37 Days to Maximum Life!* you will know how to gain control of your life, and manifest what you want. Oh, is that all? No, you will also be *awake* and *empowered* to run your show from here on out.

There is a huge advantage to industry and government in having a population of unfulfilled people. They are Drones. Drones to work in the companies. Drones to die in battle. Drones to watch TV. Drones to buy junk they don't need. Drones to eat crappy snacks that are malnourishing. Drones to run, run, run to accomplish a never-ending line of meaningless tasks. Drones to do routine tasks in plants and factories. But it is not your advantage.

Have you become seduced by any of these drone producing habits? Where one day is like any other except for a supposedly new episode of *The Young Days of Our Guiding*

Hospital? If it hasn't yet begun to bother you, it will get to you. One day you'll say, *Eeek! Is this all there is?* Dr. Schaefer has removed all obstacles in your way (by the way, most of them look a lot like you). It is angelic work, and we all should thank him for caring enough to do what it took to develop and share this secret formula.

I predict it won't be a secret much longer.

— *Anthony Dallmann-Jones Ph.D., Marco Island, Florida; author of* Primary Domino Thinking, Shadow Children, *and* The Phoenix Flight Manual.

Personal Letter from the Author

I had been going through life doing the things we humans commonly do. I created a family, a home, a career, wealth, and had lots of personal interests and hobbies. Ultimately I focused on what so many struggle toward: keeping it all in balance. And yet for me, there was a deeper question. Not a feeling of "is that all there is?" but a knowing that an un-named mystery existed, which I needed to discover and then solve. I knew there was *more!*

I had clues earlier and all through my life, and I was eager to fully unearth this mystery.

My awakening came partially through challenging what seemed to be known and expected of me by those around me. It came from challenging the status quo, and directly challenging the paradigms I had accepted from an upbringing of affluent "White Christian Midwestern American" programming. It came through events that changed my life—including divorce, bankruptcy, and several career transitions.

It was certainly a major event, and yet what came after that, for me personally, and for my three wonderful children, has been nothing short of phenomenal. I am now able to live my life with joy, with depth, and with authenticity that has brought more meaning to me than was ever possible before. I am able to observe and appreciate all that goes on around me, and I can experience inspiration and happiness in ways that are nearly indescribable.

This 37 Day Program represents a compilation of the most meaningful steps that I have taken. I offer this journey to you with the hope that you will find your way, in your world, to living and experiencing your life with the richness that I have in mine.

The amazing part is that you don't have to change anything in your outside world ... the work is all done on the inside of you. It's *all* inside you!

With love,
Rick

Introduction

Appreciation!

I have found the secret to a happy and joyful life lies in appreciation. The secret to this program is in learning to master the art of appreciation in every aspect of your life, from the smallest to the grandest.

Bliss comes from the energy of love and appreciation. When we are not blocking that love and appreciation from flowing through us from our non-physical source, from God, from the Universe, from the Angels, from Spirit ... we live in harmony and bliss.

Do you notice that there are some days that you feel that truth so clearly? You can smell the flowers, feel the cool breeze and the warm sun, you can taste food more intensely and even appreciate the carpet fibers or grass blades between your toes more. All of your senses are sharpened, and you can pause in the moment to feel and better appreciate all that is around you.

If you have ever fallen in love, you totally know what this feels like. New love allows this to happen every time. I will show you how to fall newly in love with yourself, and with your life, and you will easily experience the heightened awareness of your senses.

The opposite of this bliss is a day where you are truly discouraged. You might get discouraged by one aspect of your life and then the feeling rapidly spreads to other areas and pretty soon you have trouble finding hope in anything. These are the days that you unknowingly focused on the obstacles to love and appreciation flowing through you. You are thinking about the past that you cannot change with regret, or you are thinking about the future you cannot control with worry. Perhaps you are focused on trying to change the behavior of another person and deciding that you could truly be happy if only that other person would do something differently.

Now that we have observed these patterns, let's retrain ourselves to take control of our happiness and become creators, instead of being responders and reactors. This book will not simply be a description of the life we already know we desire. This book will give you a detailed 37 step pathway to actually get there. This path is best traveled over a period of weeks, and may be best taken multiple times, as you can hear different lessons more clearly at different points in your life. But *you will get there* if you focus and follow the path.

Most of us know what we want to do, but we don't always have the observer's perspective to be able to see clearly where we are falling short. Also, equally important, we usually don't have the tools to do it. This book contains the tools and the mechanisms that can actually *train* you in the most wonderful aspect of life: experiencing the freedom of happiness. This book will give you a mechanism to create your own happiness irrespective of your circumstances. Upon completion of this program, your level of happiness will not be dependent upon what is happening around you, but instead you will be able to create and feel at will pure joy emanating from the inside. None of this is part of our normal learning, not in the school curriculum, public education, news media, or classic parenting education. Some of us have had the gift of an inspiring teacher, coach or parent to bring this to us, but it is more the exception than the rule. We mostly live in an environment where our peers are accepting of the idea that our degree of happiness and unhappiness is outside of our own control, that we are victims of it and not agents in control of it. We hear that the economy is bad, or our bodies will fail, or life is tough, and we incorporate those thoughts and expectations, not realizing that we are actually creating that reality for ourselves by the habit of those thoughts. All of those thoughts are choices for us, we simply choose to go along with what we hear from outside of us. But we have the power to change all that!

I want to help you develop the skills to live in the moment. The key is in taking this very moment, the only one you can ever actually experience, and focusing on something that feels good *right now*. Choose something that you like, you appreciate, you can feel gratitude about—no matter how small. Do you realize how much better it feels to watch an ant crawl with your child than it does to focus on not knowing where your rent payment is going to come from next month? How much better to taste the meal you are eating right now, to let the flavor and scent fill your mouth and nose and appreciate how abundant this earth is to provide food for us, than it is to think about how your sister might have scolded you recently, and wants you to agree with her about politics or religion or parenting?

It sort of feels like "ignorance is bliss," doesn't it? Well, that *is* the secret. For most people, feeling really good is more about appreciating the goodness in something right now than it is focusing on something in the world news that is discouraging. This is simple wisdom, and probably something you have heard all your life. Your mother probably told you to "count your blessings" as a child. You have probably noticed the power of looking on the bright side. Or that attitude is everything. This wisdom has been around forever. Most of what I teach is how to naturally allow the positive energy to flow through you without blocking it or creating obstacles in your mind to the innate happiness that lies within you.

How to Use This Book

This program is designed to take about ten weeks, so if you find yourself reading this book slowly, reviewing chapters repeatedly, and pausing between the daily lessons, that is really good. Maintain the focus on that lesson throughout the day, and take a second day whenever you need it.

Extreme Thought Makeover™ will literally train you to find the positive in each and every aspect of your life, to allow you to focus on this moment in time and fully live each moment with love, appreciation, hopefulness, and empowerment!

As you go through the program, you will find you build momentum each day. You will start with the smaller aspects of your life, building confidence and momentum using the techniques taught here. Then we'll move on the bigger aspects: weight loss, disease, nutrition, parenting, and money. You will find that we take time to expose the areas of your life that you are already masterfully good at finding the positive energy around, and then moving slowly into the bigger and more difficult aspects.

You will find that by taking these "baby steps," transformation of the biggest issues in your life will then come within reach. We start with things like leaving a tip in a restaurant, finding a joyful moment from your childhood, and simply breathing; and then move on to how you see your physical appearance, putting the right nutrition into your body, dealing with a chronic disease state, and finding enough success and money to be comfortable financially.

You will find that these biggest issues will easily be within reach once you master the techniques of positive thinking around the little stuff. Eventually, you will create so much momentum around positive thinking and appreciation that joy, happiness and success will continually flow freely into your life.

Let's begin ...

The 37 Days

Most people spend their lives looking in the wrong direction. They are looking out instead of looking in.

The Pace

Okay, now, we are starting the program. Ideally, I would suggest one lesson, or "Day" per day or two. That would stretch the whole program out to six to ten weeks. That pace may seem slow, but many people like the pace of one lesson every two days. That gives them time to really digest, re-read, and sit with the content from the lesson. They can focus on the action step, and possibly spend the second day repeating the thought or the action. It seems that for most people, having the second day to review and let the lesson sink in is a really good thing.

Day 0
(Bonus Day)

Healing Energy:
Laugh

When we come into the world, we are ready to laugh, and giggle, and be tickled. We, as infants, never ever take anything too seriously (except an empty stomach or a full diaper.)

The challenge is to hold onto that lack of seriousness as we age. Laughter has been associated with increased serotonin levels and increased longevity ... which means it just feels darn good.

The Action Step for today is to laugh. Really laugh. Do whatever it takes to laugh right now. Call your favorite silly friend, read the comics, read your favorite satirist, watch a movie (*Dumb & Dumber* is always a guarantee for me, no matter where I jump into it,) or search a video clip on the internet. The net can provide you with something at a moment's notice: YouTube, NBC's *Saturday Night Live* sketches, political miscues, *America's Funniest Home Videos,* etc. Make sure it is a real belly-jiggler. Laugh till you can hardly breathe. Laugh till you cry. Go ahead while you are at it, dance and sing and don't pay any attention to who is watching, because you can only bring joy to them as well. Here's the best: try skipping and not smiling!

Now you are prepared to start this makeover. You have my permission at any time to take a break from this and laugh. Part of the end goal here is for all of us to take ourselves less seriously!

You can find links to some really funny videos on the book resources page of my website, www.rickschaefermd.com.

Angels fly because they take themselves lightly.

Day 1

Good Stuff:
Positive Images Around the House

What we see in the objects and images around us impacts our emotions. You can tell when you look at an object what emotion comes to you, and what feeling you have around it. You can tell if something gives you a negative emotion: regret, guilt, obligation, sadness, powerlessness. You can also tell if something makes you feel strong and powerful, like a picture of yourself mountain climbing, doing a water ski trick, or performing on stage as a child. Usually these are souvenirs of achievements of your past, or of really joyful moments. Put these reminders out around your home and office, and let the good feelings abound from these objects and images.

If we create a dream world from the inside out and focus on that, we will be in an emotional place consistent with that mood. Bring some of that inner world out, and into your environment. Set up images from really happy moments in your life. If you have access to trophies, certificates, or participation awards you got as a child, set them out for a bit. Then capture the feeling you had back then when you achieved the award. It might feel silly, but it will feel really good! If you are like most, it will be much easier to locate pictures, so put those out.

Make sure you do this right now, today! Another way to take the exercise a step further is to seek out all the products in your home that have positive sounding names; Joy, Glad, Fantastic, Fabulous, Cheer ... you get the idea. You'll have fun hunting for them and setting them out on display, and learning the habit of noticing the little everyday reminders of positive energy in your life.

Place these positive image objects all around your home and office. Make sure that you really feel something positive when you look at these pictures and objects. Surround yourself with things that make you feel great about who you are, and the feeling will sink in deeper and deeper. Be sure to include those pictures of you that really make you smile ... reminders from carefree times, being silly, and taking life far less seriously!

It's all for joy. Joy is the ultimate quest.
— R.S.

Inspired Personal Stories: Day 1

I get a lot of wonderful feedback from people working through the lessons in Extreme Thought Makeover™. *I am truly grateful that people are willing to share. I believe that many readers will be able to get their most helpful idea from a real life story, so I have included some here, with permission.* — R.S.

Dear Dr. Rick,

Thank you for sending me these thought makeovers. To be very honest, the first lesson worked immediately for me. I simply started putting flowers at my work station as it makes me happy. What a simple thing to do that has a positive impact on how I feel many times during the day.

— *Anila, Islamabad, Pakistan*

Hi Dr. Rick,

I don't feel very appreciated at work, and don't sense that I am on the right track for promotion. I was getting pretty down on myself and judging myself pretty harshly. I decided to take the lesson from Day 1 and really work on it. I put out a lot of really happy pictures of my kids at really adorable and innocent ages: seven, ten, twelve. It really perked me up to look at them. I think it helped me take my job situation a little less seriously, because the youthful joy certainly doesn't care about that career stuff, just having fun. Then I found some childhood pictures that showed me really happy and innocent. That just made the feeling stronger and stronger.

I have really found that I am not judging myself as harshly now, and feel a lot better at work.

— *Peter Storm, Dubuque, Iowa*

Dr. Rick,

Thanks for getting me out from under a dark cloud. This has been an eye opening process. I really like Day 1. I feel that it is very true and empowering to surround your environment with art that makes or sends positive messages and feelings. I felt really down in my bedroom

31

and started adding more and beautiful framed pictures to my room, now it's a place I love to relax in. The wisdom is so simple, and so effective.

— *Rebekah, West Bend, Wisconsin*

Day 2

Appreciation:
Go on a Rampage!

Today the focus is on bringing up the feeling and energy of appreciation as strongly as possible. Simply put your attention upon all the things you really appreciate: your favorite daily moments, things, and people. Think about them, write them down, and focus on appreciating all of the stuff that you do appreciate.

For me, I love that first taste of my favorite iced coffee drink first thing in the morning. I love seeing the sun rising, blindingly bright as I drive downtown. I love the people I care about. I love that people love me. I love discovering something new that I am drawn to. I love slipping in under a puffy warm and cozy comforter on a cool evening. I love crawling into bed on nights I don't have to set the alarm, because it really allows me to fall into the present moment, and melt into the bed. I love seeing deer walking through the yard. I love the luxury of taking a ten minute nap. I love my iPhone (oh my gosh, don't get me started on that!). I love that I am a risk-taker. I love that I am always willing to say "Yes!" I love the luxury of having an automobile, and being able to jump in and drive anywhere I want, any time I want, to be with any one I want. I love making a fresh salad from a grocer's salad bar. Wait, I love the grocer for supplying it for me. Whoa, I love the farmer who grew the lettuce for me. I love the person who invented the hot shower. I love that there is truly an endless supply of things to appreciate in this world.

You get the idea ... once you get going, it is really hard to stop. This is called a Rampage of Appreciation. I have been inspired to use this idea by the *Teachings of Abraham* audio recordings by Jerry and Esther Hicks. This focus on appreciation is the one central core principle to this book and program. Practicing this way of thinking squeezes out any space in your thoughts to be annoyed or irritated with anything in your life. Go ahead, grab a pen and paper and start writing. Keep going and going, and see what you come up with. Most importantly, recognize the feeling that comes with it. The feeling of love and appreciation for your world will become overpowering.

Is the glass half empty or half full? The answer is what you want it to be. It is totally up to you, to your imagination, and to your thoughts. And thoughts become things. So choose wisely, and practice choosing appreciation!

Hey, the better it gets, the better it gets.
— R.S.

Day 2 Writing Assignment:

Start right now, just with one thing you appreciate. Okay, maybe add just a second thing and see what happens.

_____

_____

_____

_____

_____

_____

_____

_____

_____

_____

_____

_____

Inspired Personal Stories: Day 2

Pay special attention to the story from Stephanie. Her story is a classic story about feeling like you really don't need some of these simple exercises, and then finding out that there is a special gift in the simplest of behaviors.
— R.S.

Hi Rick,

I have to comment on Day 2. I was really busy this afternoon—and in all honesty—I thought to myself, "I am a *very* positive thinking person and I already know what I appreciate in life. This is a little silly and I'm time-crunched, but I'll get it over with—I promised Rick."

I am surprised, but very happy to tell you that once I put my pen to paper and got going, I literally could not stop. I went on and on for six pages (three columns each!). I would get stumped for a minute and just one thought or feeling would come to me and that would bring a whole flood of other things to my mind that I really love or appreciate or want to do or see again. I would come to the bottom of a page and think of just one more thing that I truly love. That would start a new page and the wonderful thoughts would flow on.

The exercise made me think of a multitude of little things that give me joy or even just make me smile. It made me realize that *just thinking* about these things, not even experiencing them, lifted my spirits. It also dawned on me that I don't spend a lot of time *trying* to put or keep these things in my life. I enjoy them when they happen, but it is often almost by accident—as I don't often put them into my day "on purpose."

Many of them have always been little luxuries ... but they don't have to be. I'm going to change that. What at first seemed like a silly exercise that I was too busy to tend to, really made my day and turned out to be truly enlightening.

— Stephanie Hernandez, Marketing Consultant, Milwaukee, Wisconsin

Dear Rick,

Day 2 led to the discovery of a lot of good in a time when things were starting to go downhill for me. When the economy started to go south in 2008, I had been making fairly decent (over minimum) payments on credit card debts, trying to get back to a zero balance. Then I lost a huge amount that had been invested in stocks, and could not continue the extra payments.

Even though my financial life was miserable, I found that other parts of my life were in great shape. I was healthy. I had great friends and family. My job was still secure. I still had a roof over my head. I found that by using Day 2 and shifting my attention to the positive things going well in my life, I didn't have time to worry about money ... I was too busy "smelling the flowers!"

That is the greatest lesson for me, that the only way to actually stop thinking about something bad is to fill my mind with *other* thoughts that feel good. Thank you.
— *Jim Richmond, Racine, Wisconsin*

Hi Rick,

I believe the lesson in Day 2 is the one not to miss. I have learned how powerful it is to be grateful and have a grateful heart. I have often had my kids make a list of all of the things that they can think of to be grateful for. It is a healing exercise. We are all "appreciating" the lesson in Day 2 having been brought to us. Thanks.
— *Amy, Ann Arbor, Michigan*

Dear Rick:

I absolutely loved the Rampage of Appreciation! It really made me think of many things differently. For instance, my father and I were estranged when he died, but I had these warm and solid memories of him helping me with a solo I had for a contest. He also was a musician, so the daunting task of learning to count out the measures of the music was easy for him. He calmed me down and I won a first place medal! It was nice like that to just go on a rant about the good stuff. Thank you.
— *Carol Santos, Albany, New York*

Hi Rick,

I went through your Day 2 over a year ago, and I would like to tell you that it was so wonderful I could not stop thinking about it. I sat down on the second day early in the morning and started writing. I was shocked at how much I had to write about, and thus how much I had to be grateful for. It was a total high emotionally, I suppose like a runner's high or something.

I decided right then I wanted to have that feeling every day, so I just kept thinking about the feeling. I kept it going because I got hooked on it, hooked on the feeling, the thought of it, and the mindset. The key for me is simply pausing. Pausing throughout the day to notice all the wonderful things going on.

Hey, if it feels that good, why not feel it every day!
— *Julio, South Milwaukee, Wisconsin*

Dear Dr. Rick,

My favorite exercise has always been the Rampage of Appreciation. I wake up appreciating my life each day, and I go on a rampage of appreciation when I'm feeling stressed or in an "off" mood.

One day I was feeling frustrated because expected payment for a completed project had not yet arrived in my mailbox, and I was feeling the pinch. I could feel myself falling into an uncharacteristic place of "lack thinking." So I went on a rampage. I live from a space of abundant joy and refuse to stay in a lesser state, thus I began to appreciate things like this:

I love my little house in the woods. It's mine. I am truly fortunate and blessed to have a home. And wow, that coffee tasted especially good this morning. I sure enjoyed standing outside with my coffee as I watched the chickens run around looking for tasty morsels on the ground.

And I love the feel of my cat's fur, the way she rubs her head into my hand, essentially petting herself. And she writhes in ecstasy as I scratch along her side. And her wonderful purr motor is so loud. I can't help but relax in the presence of a purring cat!

I get to work from home instead of rushing around and spending hours just getting to and from a workplace. I get to talk to people all over the world and assist them in living their mission. And I get to write. Life doesn't get much better than this!

The eggs my chickens lay are a daily miracle to me. Every single day when I gather the eggs, I marvel at these delightful gems, each a different shade of brown, and filled with golden goodness. How amazing that I get such fresh eggs and never have to eat the "old stale ones" from the stores. I am truly blessed.

Then I looked at the patio tomato plant and noticed that three tomatoes were beginning to blush—not in embarrassment, but in impending ripeness. It won't be long before those tasty tomatoes are in a delicious salad. I love cooking and adding a blessing into everything I prepare. I also love it when someone else appreciates what I prepare.

I appreciate my body that does so many tasks without me having to manage them. What a miracle that my heart beats, food digests, and my hair grows without my active involvement. Life is positively miraculous! I've been working out more lately and am noticing increased strength and vitality, which motivates me to continue.

And even though it drives me nuts at times, I am truly grateful for the computer. It allows me to connect with people all over the world. It allows me to write my books and stories efficiently. It lets me do research so much more easily than I did back in the days of microfiche and card catalogs.

This is a much better time to be mostly blind, because there are adaptive aids and computer programs to help me hear the screen. Oh, and audio books ... I *love* audios. I am *so* incredibly grateful for sound recording.

I have so many options open to me in this time and place with the technologies and freedoms available to me. I can think, speak, vote, talk to whomever I wish and steer the course of my own life. I am focused. I am determined. I live to serve. And I am free! Now there is no room for anything but abundant joy and appreciation.

— *Ronda del Boccio, The Story Lady, Lampe, Missouri*

Day 3

A Lifetime of Learning:
Audio Education in the Bathroom

This is going to be one of the most straightforward exercises in the program. It is also, in the opinion of many, the most significant. Okay, you heard that, right? Many, many people believe this is the most significant exercise in the entire program. So I suggest you take it very seriously, and simply "Do It." Don't question it, or analyze it, or modify it. Just Do It!

The idea is simple: turn your bathroom into a university, your greatest learning environment. Here's how it works: put a CD player on the counter. Then listen to an audio book (spoken word) every single morning as you shower, shave, and groom. Play it loud enough so that you can hear it over the sound of the water in the shower. I often find that I get so lost in the teaching of whomever I am listening to, that I feel no stress about the coming day and all I might need to do. I also find that I often take the CD along with me in the car so that I can continue listening. I even find myself hoping for lots of traffic, so that I can have longer to listen. That sounds like a shift right there, doesn't it? Actually *enjoying* a traffic jam!

Choose material for your Audio Education that is going to be inspiring and foster growth for you. Consider work by Wayne

Dyer, Leo Buscaglia, Deepak Chopra, Louise Hay, Jerry and Esther Hicks, Steven Covey, Earl Nightingale, Robert Fulghum, Jack Canfield, or Joe Dispenza (just a few of my favorites). The list of who might inspire you to make a significant change in your thinking is endless. Have fun discovering and devouring new authors and new ideas each day.

The key here is consistency. Play something *every morning*. It is an amazing way to start your day. Feeding yourself mentally with inspiring thoughts can set the tone for the entire day. It provides a base for strong inner positive resistance to outside negative influences as your day progresses. It also is a great way to quiet your mind from worry, relieving your mind from racing through all the stuff that you have to do.

Using your mornings for Audio Education will provide not only a peaceful starting point to the day, but also could be the most significant factor long term to your transformation to Maximum Life! This is one of the greatest secrets to self-development: to keep learning, absorbing, and retraining your thinking by replacing everyday patterns with positive inputs. And the miracle is that it actually will not take you any time at all. Imagine that! A simple habit, taking no time, will truly transform your life. Now *that* is what this workshop is all about. Now is the time to just do it! Create your bathroom university. Start today. And never stop!

Knowing stands in the way of learning.
— R.S.

List of My Favorite Audio Resources for Day 3

Let's create a list of your favorite audio recordings. Think of your favorite positive speakers, lecturers, authors, and musicians. The key here is consistency. Play something *every morning*. It is an amazing way to start your day feeding your mind and choosing your focus.

Here are a few of my personal favorite audio-book and lecture recordings:

- *How to Really, Really, Really, Really Get What You Want* by Dr. Deepak Chopra and Dr. Wayne W. Dyer.
- *The Seven Spiritual Laws of Success* by Dr. Deepak Chopra
- *Love* by Leo Buscaglia
- *You Can Heal Your Life* by Louise Hay
- *Ask and It Is Given* by Jerry and Esther Hicks
- *The Workshop Series* by Jerry and Esther Hicks
- *The Invitation* by Oriah Mountain Dreamer
- *Secrets of the Millionaire Mind* by T. Harv Ecker
- *The 4-Hour Workweek* by Timothy Ferriss
- *Wisdom of the Ages* by Dr. Wayne W. Dyer
- *Think and Grow Rich* by Napoleon Hill
- *The Essence of Teamwork* By Pat Williams
- *10 Secrets for Success and Inner Peace* by Dr. Wayne W. Dyer
- *Meditations for Manifesting* by Dr. Wayne W. Dyer
- *Many Lives, Many Masters* by Brian Weiss, M.D.
- *The Secret* by Rhonda Byrne

Links to these wonderful recordings are available on my website at www.rickschaefermd.com.

Inspired Personal Stories: Day 3

Years ago, I had an insurance agent who was very successful, and it puzzled me as to why his car was always such a mess, cluttered with a ton of cassettes and cases. He explained that his car was his "university on wheels," and that the tapes were all sales and success training tapes. He swore that was his main secret to success ... always learning, soaking up what success techniques were working for others. I strongly considered it.

Then I met Michael S. Clouse, Editor-in-Chief at Upline Magazine, and heard his story, which is included here. I knew the contact circle that he was in, and I saw the enormous success he had. He, too, attributed his success to his constant daily learning. It sunk in, and I decided to copy their behavior.

That's it! That's the one irreversible turning point in my journey. With daily learning, you can never go back to your old habits, you just keep growing and growing. I have done it consistently for fourteen years, and I really believe it has made the biggest difference. The amazing thing is, it is one of the few exercises that can be practiced on a daily basis, and actually does not take any time out of your day to do! Imagine that!
— R.S.

Dear Rick,

I turned my bathroom into a university over ten years ago, and started listening to thirty minutes of new, inspiring information every day as I shower and shave, without exception. It has made all the difference!

When we bought our beautiful new home, my wife said, "can we finally ditch that ugly CD player sitting on the bathroom counter?" I said, "That ugly CD player is the main reason we have our new home!"
— *Michael S.Clouse, International Trainer, former Editor-In-Chief of* Upline Magazine, Seattle, Washington

Hi Rick,

If I had only *one* day that I could use, it would be Day 3, the audio education. My wife and I began listening every day to many cassettes and CDs I have accumulated over the years. We turn it up enough that we can both hear it throughout our entire "morning routines." We often stop it and talk over an idea or concept and it *always* gets my mind going in the right direction. What a way to start the day! By the time I get to work, I am so charged and positive that I really think it has been one of my main keys to success. There is no room for any negative.

This ended up changing my habits in many areas. Like you, I often take the CD with me in the car to continue listening. I recently bought an iPod so I can also now listen while mowing the lawn. I really think the key to this day is the first thing in the morning part. It makes it easier to get out of bed in the morning, too!

— *Bill Driscoll, VP of Training and Dealer Development, DeTech Fire-Sense Technologies, Saukville, Wisconsin*

Dear Rick,

My life was great a few years ago. I had seven mall stores and did fourteen trade shows a year in major cities, making me a great income. The industry then shifted to more online sales, and the economy in general shifted downward, and my business struggled. I was forced to close most of my stores and a 5000 square foot distribution center. I almost lost everything.

The only thing that I did not lose was "hope." After reading Day 3, I saw the potential power of this early morning education. I bought and downloaded tips and lessons on how I could improve my business revenue by some of the major marketers in my industry. The best part was, whatever I was learning early morning while showering, I usually continued listening to in the car on the way to the office. I arrive at the office eager to implement an idea every day.

It has really helped my focus shift from just working in the business to working *on* the business, and creating growth. I incorporated many of these marketing tips successfully, and indeed, have much to be hopeful for. It's a simple habit that I made in my life which has had a huge impact on my business and personal life.

— *Sonny Ahuja, Owner, Grand Perfumes, Milwaukee, Wisconsin*

Day 4

Productivity:
Create a Five Things List

I want to help you be more productive every day. This course isn't focused on productivity, however, being productive and accomplishing a few significant tasks each day feels really good, increases self-esteem, and brings joy ... and that *is* what this course is about!

What stands in our way of focus and productivity each day is *distraction*. This productivity exercise is a simple technique to quiet the distractions for a while in order to gain clarity and focus. Here's how it works: each evening, write down the five most important things that you want to accomplish the next day. Make sure that these tasks are meaningful and significant to you. They may have to do with personal, health, travel, family, business ... whatever it is that you value. Make sure to make them significant for you. Choose things that will leave you with a good feeling when you put your head on the pillow tonight. Now prioritize them, numbering one through five with the most important first.

Okay, now here is the revolutionary productivity technique: first thing the next morning, sit down and start working on number one. Do not answer the phone. Do not check email.

Do not look up or do any other small task (except refilling your coffee cup) until it is complete. Once number one is complete, immediately start on number two. Do not answer the phone. Do not check email. Do not look up or do any other small task until it is complete. There you have it ... the secret to productivity!

When your head hits the pillow tonight, you will know that you accomplished the two most meaningful and important tasks you set out to do today. It will provide a great feeling of satisfaction, accomplishment, capability, and joy. Usually with this intentional focus, I find I can finish the first two tasks before 10:00 a.m. That's amazing! It gives me that feeling of joy and accomplishment for the entire rest of the day.

It all seems so simple doesn't it? That's how you know it is right. The best solutions are always simple.

Have a wonderful day.

Note: if you would like to read about how I was inspired to incorporate this genius idea into my life, do an internet search on "the $25,000 idea" by the great master of motivation Earl Nightingale.

I'm fixing a hole where the rain gets in and stops my mind from wandering.
— The Beatles, "Fixing a Hole"

Inspired Personal Stories: Day 4

Dr. Rick ,

I've always been a doer. I used to have a massive to-do list, with fifty or more items on it, which can be really daunting. I would look at the list and think, "I can kick off twelve of these real fast so that I can get it from fifty to thirty-eight." What I would notice is I was constantly spilling over to the next day, so there'd be five items left, twenty items left, or whatever.

That felt as if I wasn't accomplishing enough, which was really frustrating. And so, after reading Day 4 with the emphasis on just the top five things that you are really going to accomplish, before anybody else is up and moving, and emailing, and calling, it really changed the landscape of my day. It has now allowed me to feel every day like I've accomplished and feel really, really good about it.

The other part of that whole five thing principle is tackling the hardest one first. If there's a to-do item there that's going to take an hour, instead of knocking out the other four and then having this last one, getting that first big one done helps you look at the other four like, "this is a piece of cake." Prioritizing the biggest task first I think had an even bigger impact than just really dialing in five major things to get done on a daily basis.

It is all about how you feel, because the better you feel the better you are, the better you are to other people, the more productive that you can be. I think I do better work and am a better person in general when I have this sense of accomplishment day in and day out.

It's really amazing. It gives you a chance to be ahead of schedule all day long. So then you just feel like you've got all this bonus time and that's been really important for me. I really believe it's allowed me to go from twelve–sixteen hour workdays to to sometimes just six hours. That gives me more time doing what I want to do. That's a great feeling!
— *Larry Morgan, St. Paul, Minnesota*

Hi Dr. Rick,

Here's the way Day 4 worked for me. On the morning I did this exercise the first time, I wrote out all of the things I had to get done.

The list was huge, way past five, and filled with stuff that can't be done in a day like "lose 100 lbs." But it made me prioritize my life in segments like personal stuff, work stuff, family stuff. That was cool. From there, I broke things down into more manageable tasks. So, instead of "lose 100 lbs.", it turned into "go on the treadmill for thirty minutes." That was a big breakthrough on its own because I always looked at things on an "end in mind" kind of thinking and not with all of the steps needed to accomplish the end goal.

Setting a structured work environment has always been a double-edged sword for me. I need it to stay focused, but at the same time, if I don't have flexibility in it, I hate it. The list I make out each day allows for both. I also have been taught by others that the most successful people in the world schedule their play time into their days just to stay on schedule. So if they want to golf, they schedule it in. If they want to go to the spa, they schedule it in and then get back on task. I like that.

I'm accomplishing more than I ever have. I'm watching less TV, which was one of my weaknesses, and I enjoy trying my best to finish everything on the list everyday. There's nothing worse than writing down a task from the day before on the new day's sheet. Especially when you could've gotten it done.
— *Jim Gehrke, Executive Greens, Milwaukee, Wisconson*

Hi Rick,

I have found a secret productivity tool! A dog. Yes, a puppy! In November of 2009, I went and got a puppy, and named him Red. It was something I had wanted for years, to get a dog again.

So puppies like to get up early ... and I really welcome him greeting me in the morning so I can care for him. So there I am at 5:40 every morning after taking care of Red, wondering what to do with this early morning time. Well, I remembered your program and went back to your Day 4, the List. I realized this was my chance to get a couple of the most important tasks of the day done. So I started following the list perfectly. I would fill in the five things in the evening, and go to bed knowing that by 8 a.m., I would be way ahead on my day.

Sure enough, 5:30 I'm up, and 5:40 with a total mindset to start cranking out these five things as soon as I can. I like to take on what I call my hardest thing on my list first. It always gets done, and usually the second one as well. You are right when you say it feels like you've accomplished a whole day's work by 10 a.m., I totally have that.

And as I say, as a little residual, it makes me look at Red in a different way. You know, somebody easily could look at him and say, "aw come on man, why you waking me up, I want to sleep," but I look at it like Red is the guy that gets me started and gets my day going for me. And I already love him to death, but I love him even more because of that.

— *Lena, Chicago, Illinois*

Day 5

Appreciating Others:
Send a Card Daily

I promised you more happiness in your life through the journey of this 37 Day Program. The shortest pathway to a feeling of happiness is finding something to appreciate, right now! Today's exercise is a way for you to immerse yourself in the feeling of appreciation at the start of every day.

In a quiet moment in the early part of your day, sit down and send a card to someone through the mail. Make it an unexpected card of appreciation. Just choose someone you know and write a few words of appreciation to them: it can be a family member, a friend, coworker, acquaintance, neighbor, or even the barista at your local coffee shop who really makes your day. Take this time early in the day and let them know how they impact your life in a positive way, however simple. A smile, a favorite phrase, a silly joke, whatever ... let them know that your life is better for them being in it. Imagine their delight and surprise in opening and reading the note that you are sending.

That can have a huge impact. There have been lives that have been changed, and lives that have been saved, with just a kind word or a card.

Man's common desire is the craving to be loved, to be recognized, to be "seen," to be appreciated. It is so simple to send a note, and so huge to receive one. Equally importantly, the sender of the card (you) will get a good feeling as well. There is an amazing story in the 4th Course of *Chicken Soup for the Soul* by Canfield and Hansen called "You don't bring me flowers anymore." It speaks of this act of giving, of sending out appreciation, actually saving a life. It is my all time favorite story from the series.

Send the cards out any way you like: old stationery, a legal pad, sticky notes with a stamp on them, anything. Many use a relatively new service online called SendOutCards. If you like working on the computer and internet, it makes this sending process ultra simple. There is a link to the SendOutCards site with a video tour on my home page www.rickschaefermd.com.

But be sure to do this once a day, ideally early in the morning. It is easy, simple, and takes less than five minutes.

Be aware—this practice may cause you to unexpectedly feel joy and lightness on a daily basis! One sender describes the feeling saying, *"It fills me with magic and opening and life each time I do it. And it spreads love vibration into the world."*

People will forget what you said, and people will forget what you did, but they will never forget how you made them feel.
— Maya Angelou

Inspired Personal Stories: Day 5

Please pay special attention to the story by Kody Bateman. He took the inspiration of "acting on promptings" and "sending unexpected cards of appreciation" and founded a multimillion-dollar company. His company, SendOutCards, facilitates the sending of traditional "by mail" greeting cards by way of a server-based internet program. Now there are hundreds of thousands of cards of appreciation criss-crossing the globe because of Kody. What a majestic legacy he has. In fact, he was my personal inspiration for this day's lesson.

He also has one of the all time most moving stories about the power of a single card of appreciation.
— R.S.

Hi Rick,

I learned early in life never to ignore a "prompting," an inclination to do something important. Twenty years ago, I made a promise to my brother that I would never again ignore a prompting. In the late '80s, I had just accepted a job in New York City and we were leaving home in Salt Lake City to move on to my new career. We said goodbye to our friends and family and got in the car to leave. "Like it was yesterday, I remember getting in our car and looking out at the field next to my parents' house. My brother, Kris, was moving some vehicles around. At that moment I had a prompting that I needed to slow down and take the time to run over and give my big brother a hug and say goodbye. I ignored that prompting. We jumped in the car, honked, waved and drove away."

Two months later, in a small apartment in New Jersey, I learned that my brother had been killed in a work accident. This event was a defining moment in my life and the driving force behind starting Send-OutCards, a company that makes it easy for people to stay in touch with greeting cards and gifts.

"I made a promise to my brother that night that I would never ignore a prompting again. I also promised that I would help as many people as I could to act on their promptings to reach out to others.

This moment changed my life forever. I immediately began my journey to not only learn the power of promptings, but to find ways to make it simple for people to act on them. I will never forget the powerful impact this experience had on my life. I received the message loud and clear that my mission in life was to act on my promptings and help others do the same."

— *Kody Bateman, founder and CEO, SendOutCards, author of* Promptings: Your Inner Guide to Making a Difference.

Hey Rick,

I wanted to add one of my favorite card stories.

I begin every day by celebrating life. One Saturday morning, I was heading to the office and thinking of whom I could send a card to that day. The first person that came to mind was a lady by the name of Pat Chase. Pat takes care of the music at the church I attend. *Cool*, I thought, *when I get to the office I will send Pat a card.* I got to the office, immediately opened up my greeting card system, and looked up Pat Chase. I already had her name and address saved along with about 1,700 other names and addresses at the time. I went to the online greeting card catalog, went to the motivational section, and found a card that said, "Beauty" on the front. The inside right of the card said, "Things are beautiful if you love them." This was the perfect greeting card. I typed a message on the left panel saying:

Pat,
Just a quick note to let you know I appreciate all you do for us at the church. You make music beautiful, and I am a better person for it.
Your friend,
Kody

Then I simply pushed the send button. This sent that card over the Internet to our printers, where thousands of cards just like it are printed, stuffed, stamped, and mailed every day.

About two weeks went by. I showed up at church, and Pat Chase walked up to me. She said, "Kody, can I speak to you?" We stepped over to a corner where she told me the following story.

"First of all, I would like to thank you for the card you sent me," she began.

"You are very welcome, Pat, and I want you to know I really meant it," I said. "My life is blessed with the beautiful music you provide."

"I would like to tell you what happened the day I received that card," Pat said. "It was a Thursday morning. I woke up feeling really discouraged and down, especially about my assignment at the church. You know, I don't remember the last time someone thanked me for what I was doing. In fact, the only thing I could remember were the complaints.

I walked into my front room that morning and picked up the receiver of my phone. I began to dial the number of the church leader. I was about to let him know that I would no longer be doing the music at the church. But something told me to hang up the phone and walk out to get the mail first. So I hung up the phone, walked out to the mailbox, and the only piece of mail in that mailbox was a greeting card from you. I opened the card, read it, and openly wept at the mailbox."

Her final words were priceless. She said, "Kody, thank you so much for that greeting card. I will never forget you for how you made me feel on that day."
— *Kody Bateman*

Dear Rick,

I am so grateful. Sending out the cards has had an amazing impact on the family and friends I have so far sent them to and I love doing it. I will often add motivational quotes, or just say I love you, whatever feels good to me in the moment. It has really been appreciated.

This message came to me at the perfect time. I was really craving to make deeper connections in so many relationships, and now I feel like I have begun a journey that could last a lifetime, which feels really wonderful.

Love, light and abundance.
— *Janet Boyd, United Kingdom*

Dear Rick,

I just wanted to share a personal story with you about the power that sending cards to people can have by leaving a lasting imprint on hearts.

One of my children had some dark times during high school, and became caught up in a world of alcohol and drugs. It was such a difficult time for us all because it is so hard to watch someone you love go through that, and not know if they'll ever find their way back to themselves, or to you.

We were lucky. We had a family intervention and it worked. I whisked her off to a rehab center several states away, and there I left her. That too was hard—not knowing who was going to care for her; trusting her safety, recovery and emotional experience into the hands of complete strangers. She was ready to leave her former life behind, but stepping into this new environment with no clue what was about to happen was frightening, and she was all alone.

I took your lesson about sending a card daily to heart, and I sent her a card every single day she was there—for seven weeks. I told her how much I believed in her, and that she could believe in herself and that she would be successful. And sent my love. Some cards were just to make her laugh. Some days I sent her two or three cards, just because it felt right.

One and a half years has passed since that time, and she has maintained her sobriety with strength and courage. And in that time, she has told me how precious those cards were for her and how much they meant to her. She looked forward to receiving them each day and the messages of love and belief affected her deeply. And she has saved every single one of them.

— *April Jensen, Manistee, Michigan*

Day 6

Self-Love:
Your Childhood Picture

Strengthening our own self-love is the pathway to having more unconditional love to offer to others, and the first step is to begin to see ourselves as worthy and full of potential.

Today, find a picture of a child that you love at a young, tender, and precious age. It can be your own child, a friend's child, a nephew, niece, neighbor, or a child you've never met. Now stare into the picture and think about what you wish for this child as they grow. Think about the worthiness you wish them to feel. Do it for as many children as you choose, as often as you like.

Hold on to that feeling. Next, find a picture of yourself at a young age that shows you in a state of happiness. Ideally, pick a favorite age or one of your all-time happiest moments. For many, a lot of these most joyful memories take place between the ages of seven and thirteen.

Looking back, my most carefree age was ten. Carefree times, good friends, and tons of playfulness were characteristic of my general state of being. Certainly I didn't take anything too seriously at that age. Today, my personality still naturally and intentionally carries with it much of that ten-year-old. And it comes out the most when I am truly happy.

Take that picture of you in your childhood and stare deeply into it. Ask yourself what you would wish for *this* child as they mature ... the worthiness you would wish for them to feel as they grow. Imagine the possibilities, the potential ... the whole universe opens up at their fingertips. State aloud that you would wish for them to follow their heart and find happiness and joy in everything that they do. Wish for them to find something that makes them come alive, because the world so needs people that have come alive.

Hold on to that feeling. Really let what you wish for that child sink in. Now, take a few moments to realize ... that child is *you*! That beautiful child of unlimited possibilities still lives in you. Allow yourself to receive the wishes that you visualized earlier. Keep this picture in plain sight so that you can be reminded regularly of what you wish for *you*.

Allowing this good-natured, full-of-potential vision of yourself to penetrate your thinking will strengthen your self-love. And don't forget ... the more love *you* possess, the more you can give to others!

Treat yourself at least as well as you treat others.
— R.S.

Inspired Personal Stories: Day 6

Dr. Rick

I work with a consulting company. As I was preparing for last minute changes to a recent seminar, I had a great idea to utilize pieces of your course. Since I was talking about self-image, I had asked everyone attending to bring a couple of pictures of themselves at various times in their lives. This was wonderful for them to trigger memories and to begin the dream again. The difference for them was the conscious experience of the feelings that came over them. It was far more powerful than me just telling them about the idea. Thank you.
— *Jasper Stanford, LifeSuccessPros.com, Fallston, Maryland*

Hey Rick,

In Day Six, Self-Love, you explain the necessity of being selfish in a way that is quite understandable. The practical exercise is great. I used it today with the mother of one of my clients today. She never ever takes time for herself. She just does what her daughter approves of—instead of the other way around. It was wonderful, and it really seemed to sink in to put her attention on herself, from out of herself looking at her childhood "self"! Thanks.
— *Johanna Lopez, Quakertown, Pennsylvania*

Dear Dr. Rick,

Your lessons on self-love have come at a very opportune time in my life, because it seems that until I get a lot better at loving myself, I won't be able to move forward in the ways that I deeply desire!

So, I found a picture of myself when I was six years old; put it in a frame and kept it next to my computer. Every time I work, or do anything at all on the computer, I see the picture of that sweet, young face and those innocent eyes looking out at me.

It occurred to me that what I felt for that little girl when I looked in her eyes is the same as what I feel with all children—that I wish for all good things in life to come to her. It was a really cool feeling to experience, and gave me such a sense of tenderness and hope for her.

Once I really thought about it, I became aware of the fact that the little girl is me! How funny to say that it had seemed like it was some-one else, but it's true. Then, I realized that there was something else I wanted to do for her and that was to let her know that I will protect her from harm and I will hold her close to me always, safe and loved.

You know what I realized? That I am the only one who can protect her and rescue her; but also, I am the only one who can hurt her now! I am the one who can make her feel criticized or judged or scolded, by doing those things to myself. So I found the inspiration to *not* treat my-self poorly in my awareness of loving and caring for that young girl who just happens to be me.

What a great idea, and what a great experience! I won't let *anyone* harm her, and that includes *me*. Thanks so much Dr. Rick!
— *Jillian, Eau Claire, Wisconsin*

Day 7

Finding New Love:
Personal Attributes List

Welcome to Day 7! You have made it through the first week of your Extreme Thought Makeover™. Let's celebrate by seizing today as a great opportunity for another Rampage of Appreciation. Today's focus and exercise is similar to Day 2, but we are shifting our attention from the things around us to things within us.

Begin by writing a list of all of the things that you love about yourself. Take ten completely focused minutes and allow no interruptions. Once you get started, the positive energy will build and build until you become overwhelmed with the feeling of appreciation of self. This sense of self-appreciation is really an essential step leading to joy, and to loving others more fully. You already logically know that you cannot give away what you do not possess. Therefore, to love others well, you must first love yourself well. To be accepting of others, you must first be accepting of self. To admire, to care for, to nurture others ... well, you get the idea.

So close the door, turn off the phone ringer, grab a pen and paper, and start writing. Start small, and build ... and build ... and build. Think about all of your great qualities and even physical attributes that you appreciate about yourself.

As examples, consider one of my personal Rampages of Self-Appreciation to get you going:

I love that I am bold and confident. I love that I can bench press 180. I love that I am a dog-lover. I love that I am a cat-lover. I love that I am not afraid of spiders. Or thunder. Or lightning. I love that I am such a good model for my kids with their future careers. I love the look of my forearms. I love that my mom taught me good table manners. I love that I can play "Lady Madonna" on the piano. I love that I have such a balanced view of money, and religion, and politics. I love that I know all the words to "Bennie and the Jets." I love that I often act like a ten-year-old.

Have a blast with your Rampage! Now remember, on a daily basis, to write one positive personal attribute on paper to allow this loving feeling of self-appreciation to continue to grow and shift your attention within you.

Which is greater, to love or to be loved? Resoundingly, it is a tie!
— R.S.

Inspired Personal Stories: Day 7

Hi Rick,

I have three children, all of whom are adorable and wonderful people. Through their growing years we had many, many fun times and memorable experiences. And, we also had some challenging times, as any family does.

For me, my youngest child brought the greatest challenges to me. She was, and is, a sweet and huge hearted person; and for several years she was rebellious and contrary and insolent—yes, a huge challenge.

We had many interactions that were difficult; more that were difficult than the ones that were good feeling. I had many moments when I felt like a failure as a mom, and also so much sadness because I couldn't find a way to connect with this daughter of mine whom I loved with all my heart—loved in way that words cannot capture.

Over time the situation shifted, and she returned to being the person that she truly is inside. That has been a precious gift. And, it has given me the chance to reflect on the times that we were closer to each other, and to wonder if there was some common element present during those times.

I have been able to see the common thread within those times; and I realize now that it all came back to *me*—how I was treating myself. I realized that when I was already appreciating something about myself, she was able to give me a hug; or just be pleasant! When my focus was on something that I was enjoying about myself, I was in a lighter emotional place and that was when the girl whose heart is wide open showed up! The opposite turned out to be true, also—when I was blaming or criticizing myself, she was nowhere to be found. When I didn't like myself, she didn't like me much either ... what a perfect Law of Attraction reflection. In those "down" times, we were unable to connect with each other in any positive way at all.

It was quite an eye opening awareness to have. I wondered how much easier it might have been if I had realized this sooner; and then I realized that second guessing myself was the opposite of what brought the happier interactions to me. So I stopped second guessing myself!

As I keep remembering this concept, I play with it more and more to see what happens. To my delight, I have discovered that the more I appreciate anything about myself, the more fun I have with other people. Anyone! Even the clerks at the grocery store respond playfully, even before I get to their counter. They see me coming, look at my face, and then ask me what it is that's making me so happy. And they're already smiling before I give an answer. I love it!!

It seems so clear, and really, very easy. When I decide to like something, anything, about me, good stuff happens. How simple can it get! And I have my wonderful daughter to thank for it. She was, and is, a genius spiritual teacher! My reflections have allowed me to realize that what she offered to me was of incredible value. My appreciation for the lesson, and the reflection, is immense. And I have never forgotten it.

— *Judy Corkle, Lighten Up Coaching, Chicago, Illinois*

Dear Dr. Rick,

As we walk by a mirror, most of us look and find fault for something. It could be our hair, our freckles, our teeth. As we continue to beat ourselves up, we are subconsciously creating a cloud of negativity around us; a cloud that only gets darker and darker. I know, I was in that storm many years ago. I used to beat myself up on a regular basis. As if I really needed more abuse, especially from the only person I'll live with for the rest of my life.

When practicing "Dr. Rick's" Extreme Thought Makeover™ Program, including Day 7 of "Finding New Love" on a daily basis, the clouds gradually disappear, making room for a new sense of joy. The bonus is, there's no need to keep asking everyone else, "Does this look okay?" or "How is my hair?" You already know! You feel deep inside that you are worthy, joyful and beautiful. Sometimes you may not even look at yourself when you pass by a mirror. You soar!

Today I wake up and the first thing I do when I look in the mirror is say, "Good Morning Goddess!" I breathe and send a big hug to *me* lifting my vibration even higher. What a wonderful start to the day! The dark, ugly clouds from the past are lifted and it feels like the sun is always shining inside. When I walk by the mirror, I look at what I love about me; my eyes, my hair, my smile. I think about my endless capacity to love, to share joy, and to forgive, especially myself! When you be-

gin to truly love and accept yourself, that love and acceptance naturally ripples down and flows to everything else in your life.
— *Teri Williams, Chief Visionary Officer, TheBlissNetwork.com, Birmingham, Michigan*

Day 8

Charity:
Give a Gift Daily

Giving unconditionally can bring a lot of joy, happiness, love, and appreciation into your life. Think of how good it feels when you have a gift for someone that they are *really* going to love. What we can do today is bring some of that positive energy into every single day of the year.

As usual, it is a simple Action Step: give a gift every day. There is no need to make it costly, just thoughtful. There are two great ways that I have discovered to be reminded on a daily basis to give.

One way is to give the same thing away every day as a routine. It can be a flower, a hand-written note, a $5 bill, or even a hug. Don't let the day pass until you have given out your un-expected "gift hug."

The second way is to give a gift whenever you visit someone. Always! Chocolates, flowers, a poem, or even a kind word delivered with care can be enough.

The cost of the gift is never in question, it is the feeling around giving and receiving that is important. I believe the habit of giving daily, unexpectedly, can be something that will grow to huge proportions some day. Over time, if you are consciously giving every single day, it can only lead to bigger and bigger things. You may someday be provided such abundance that you will be able to give huge gifts as easily and regularly as you gave small ones.

Just to get it started, pick one gift today: a flower, a poem, a $5 tip, or a hug. Give it away unexpectedly to someone that has caught your attention in a positive way. If it feels good, continue on a daily basis.

What you keep to yourself, you will lose. What you give away, you will feel forever.

Inspired Personal Stories: Day 8

Dr. Rick,

I would like to share a story about gifting. It has really helped me shift my energy and emotion. Recently I completed a three month contract for a client that had a discretionary bonus clause upon completion. Well, the contract went absolutely as well as could be, perfect, without any obstacles. I actually provided service well beyond what was required, and delivered a final product that far exceeded my client's expectation. My client was rumoring all along that he would honor the discretionary clause to it's fullest, which would have resulted in approximately a $10,000 bonus to me at the end.

Well, Dr. Rick, and you might have seen this one coming, when we wrapped up the last detail of the contract, he did not back up his promise. Instead he told a story of how tough it was financially right now, and that he had lost some money in the stock market, and just couldn't "afford" to pay the full bonus. He opted to give me only ten percent of the bonus, $1,000. I was really hurt, and felt betrayed to a large extent, and manipulated.

I stared at that $1,000 check and could not find positive energy in it. Okay, I understand that $1,000 is a lot of money, and could be celebrated, but unfortunately what it represented to me was that it was $9,000 lacking. I needed to do something to shift my energy around this check. Just then, Day 8 from your program came to mind: Charity. Of course, I would give the money away! So I found two people to give $500 each to who were really, really wanting financial help with purchases very important to them.

Wow, sure enough, the energy about that $1,000 completely shifted, and it is still filling me up with the abundant feeling of the legacy it has. I am thankful that I was able to go through this experience. I am so wonderfully impressed that by following such a simple idea, charity, that I could totally transform my feeling about a bonus from disappointment, betrayal and lack to generosity, love and abundance. That small $1,000 bonus was transformed into two giant $500 gifts. Thank you.

— *Karina Matthews, Madison, Wisconsin*

Hey Rick,

I love having plants around the home—one of my favorites is the Spider Plant! Put around your computer, they absorb radiation and purify the air. I also find green to be a very relaxing and healing colour.

My friend Lisa commented on how lovely they looked, so I decided to let her have one. She was overjoyed and I got as much pleasure from giving a small gift in appreciation for having such a good friend.

The next day she asked if I had another that she could give to her mum, who also loved plants. Of course, I was only too pleased. I also gave one to my friend Christina and a couple to my lovely mum and dad, who are always so generous.

About this time, it occurred to me that if I continued giving them all away, eventually there would be none left! But the Universe has ways of showering you with abundance and a few months later my actions were rewarded ten-fold.

The few remaining plants I had started to reproduce more plants. In fact, as fast as I was potting the new Spider plants, more were appearing! So much so, that I am now *having* to give them away before they take over my office.

— *Honey Malone, Nutritionist, Herbalist, mother of three, United Kingdom*

Dear Dr. Rick,

I've always loved to give things to people, but I really like the concept of giving every single day. When I first read this lesson, the only gift ideas I could think of were gift cards. After more thought, I realized I could have a bigger impact if I gifted somebody with something that would feel absolutely amazing when they came in contact with me. And so I decided that my mission would be to give joy to people.

I help people through divorce and financial issues, so I often meet with people in my business who are in very difficult situations and it is hard to encourage them to think positively. But I've worked on figuring out how to have people walk away from meeting with me and realize that they have their whole life ahead of them, full of opportunity. And so when I can meet with people and then see them leave with a big smile on their face and be motivated and inspired, that to me is a more special gift than anything else I can give. And I still give other things, like buying lunch or coffee, but it doesn't have the same kind of effect.

I'm actually going to keep track of what I experience through that joy-giving so I can look back to see what great energy I'm producing daily.
— *Dante, Grand Rapids, Michigan*

Hi Rick,

Yesterday as I was returning from a doctor's appointment, I decided to do a favor for a friend of mine who recently hurt and disappointed me. My initial reaction was to ignore him and punish him for his betrayal to me. But instead, I chose to do a "180."

I decided to bless and overcome negativity with positive energy. The great part was that I felt positive and excited. This was a great gift I was giving myself. I had transformed a negative attitude into one that put such a sweet smile on my face that others commented on it. I couldn't undo what had happened, but I could have an impact on what might happen in the future. I would rather have something positive happen than to deepen the rift between me and my friend.

The second positive was that my friend was most appreciative. I "made his day" and I made a stronger bond in the friendship that exists between us. The third positive was that while I was en route to do this favor for my friend, I received a phone call from someone who I had helped out previously by providing free treatment for her sister who had no insurance. She told me she had just come into some money and offered to send me on a trip if I would like to go. How sweet is that?
— *Dr. Ray Lueck, Family Care Psychological Servies, Wauwatosa, Wisconsin*

Day 9

Affirmations:
Posting Positive Messages

On Day 1, you placed positive images and objects all around your home and office environments. Today I'd like you to put up some very specific signs in your home. Consider what you are most grateful for, and then put up specific reminders for yourself of these people and things.

As an example, if you have kids, perhaps you could place a sign on the door coming in from the garage that states: "Within this home live the most spectacular children on the planet." Or perhaps you could post a sign on the bathroom mirror stating: "A more perfect child has never been born." When you pull your car in the garage, perhaps there could be a sign that states: "Welcome to the home of the most wonderful, amazing spouse on this Earth, and s/he is madly in love with *me*!"

Dream up anything. Put an "I love my kitchen" magnet on the fridge. Or, on the door to the family room: "The most comfortable room in the world." These are all statements that reflect your true feelings when you are immersed in appreciation ... gratitude for where you live, what you have, and with whom you live. Don't be afraid to dramatize the positive feelings you have, and enjoy them! Lavishing this positive attention on the things you are grateful for can only make that feeling of appreciation grow.

Have fun reminding yourself to return to the daily posture of joyous appreciation!

Nothing is more important than that you FEEL good.
— R.S.

Inspired Personal Stories: Day 9

Dear Dr. Rick,

I wanted to share a story about a simple affirmation that I believe has had a profound impact on my son. He is seventeen now and entering his senior year of high school. Two years ago, I observed a contradiction: he was a tremendous independent learner, studying on his own topics to great intensity and mastery. But in school, where he was asked to focus on topics of other people's desire (mostly the school board in the public education system), he performed only slightly above average. This was a far cry from the intense mastery he attained outside of school.

As a college graduate myself, I realized that traditional education can only take a person so far, and that eventually all learning comes independently. I wanted to encourage and inspire him. More importantly, I wanted him to recognize the tremendous life learning skill he had obtained, and not be discouraged by the school's lack of recognition of his independent-learning ability.

Well, he *was* a teenager, and rather than try to explain all that and risk getting too preachy, I decided to place an inspiring statement within his view. I taped a typewritten note to the inside of his bedroom door simply saying, "Don't Let School Stand in the Way of a Good Education." To my delight, he left the note up. He rarely spoke of it, but I can tell you he is a better person for it.

He is completely at peace with his grades, has the utmost confidence in his learning ability, and outscored his predicted standardized ACT test by over 60%. He has his sight set on college, and is very proud to be "not average."

I believe positive statements and affirmations can have a profound effect on us, whether we are speaking them, or simply seeing them. And thank goodness for me, even if they are posted by a parent ... a very proud parent.

— *Paul C., Whitefish Bay, Wisconsin*

Hi Dr. Rick,

I would like to tell you about "Charlie." Charlie was in one of the job networking Mastermind groups that I facilitate. He was one of eight members that were introduced to a different way of approaching the job search process.

One of those principles begins with Stephen Covey's, "Start with the end result in mind." Each participant writes down what their "Successful Employment" looks like to them, by describing it in detail, on their "Employment Card." Neville, the author, writes that you want to then work from the perspective that it is already completed, instead of working towards it.

When it comes to resumes, our approach is "Do you believe it will get you in the door?" If not, work on it until you *believe* it will.

One meeting, Charlie started reporting his successes. He talked about how he met someone who reviewed his resume and made a suggestion he really like and implemented. He then handed out his "new" resume with a smile and glow of *belief*. Within two weeks, Charlie had his first interview with the company that ultimately hired him. He was the first from the group to find "Successful Employment" because he *believed* he would.

After he reported his new employment, he talked about how he visualized his employment from the first day he wrote out his Employment Card.

What do you believe? About your job? About your job search? About your Life? Whatever you believe, so shall it be.
— *Jeffrey R. Percival, perc-ent.com, Milwaukee, Wisconsin*

Hi Rick,
Thank you for making this recommendation. I find the positive is always more powerful. I love the below Louise Hay affirmations:
"All is well in my world."
"Everything goes right for me."
— *Jean S. Elm Grove, Wisconsin*

Day 10

Detachment:
Toss Something Out

In order to achieve a feeling of total security and total freedom, it is necessary to let go of our attachment to physical things. Detachment holds the wisdom of uncertainty and possibilities. When you embrace uncertainty, you will find security. When you embrace possibilities, you will find freedom. A simple first step toward detachment is letting go of small physical items. Let's get started!

Today, get rid of one thing. It could be a pair of shoes, a knick-knack, or an old souvenir glass. Just pick one thing and give it away, recycle it, throw it away, or put it in the garage for a future "Give-Away Day" (see below for more on this idea). This physical action is a representation of clearing mental space for clear and creative thinking, and when made habit, can transform the way you interact with your physical and emotional environment profoundly. Think about the stuff you have that clutters your living space. Where to begin? Well, you could start a "five year rule" for clothing, for example. That's an easy one: if you haven't worn it for five years, you will definitely not miss it! Perhaps even a two-year rule? One year? Just because you haven't exercised your throwing-away muscles in a while, doesn't mean you can't start somewhere ... like with a coffee mug from the back of the cupboard. Don't worry that it is in great condition or that you paid good money for it, it is the getting-rid-of energy that will be far more valuable to you, and the value will come back to you many fold.

As your physical space becomes more and more clear, you will find that previously cluttered areas give way to empty space, allowing for a mental shift from the focus of "what is" to the focus of endless possibilities. Your living space will become a blank canvas upon which anything can be created, in any moment.

De-cluttering feels like clearing your stuff, but it is actually clearing your mind. Jumbled, crowded thoughts will give way to clarity and focus. Creative energy will emerge in the space vacuum you have created for it. Your new thinking will have the room it needs to be powerful and inspiring!

A continuation of this exercise for the future is to have a "Give-Away Day." Fill the garage bit by bit with all the stuff you have uncluttered through your new daily attitude of de-taching. When it really starts to pile up, call your friends and invite them to come and get all your stuff. They will go crazy and really create a great memory for themselves and for you. Plus, the objects themselves will have a much more useful and vibrant life in their new home.

In detachment lies the wisdom of uncertainty, and in uncertainty lies freedom from our past: from the known. It is also where limitless possibilities are found. Stay open to the possibilities by manifesting an attitude of detachment in your physical environment today.

Simplicity is the most difficult thing to achieve in this world; it is the last limit of experience and the last effort of genius.
— George Sand

Inspired Personal Stories: Day 10

Hi Dr. Rick,

Of all the lessons covered in *Extreme Thought Makeover*™, my favorite is Day 10, Detachment. I *love* to de-clutter, I get a charge out of exercising my "throwing away muscles." There are times I get attached to things that no longer serve me, but when I take a deep breath and actually begin moving through the process, I feel sooooo much better. Detachment takes on many forms; not only does it get rid of "things" just taking up space in my physical environment, it helps me with mental housekeeping as well. If you don't let go of the old, you can't make room for the new.

There was a time that it was difficult for me to let go of old outdated inventory from my own business (I design and print T-shirts), but after sorting out the tug of war I seemed to be having about letting go of something that I put my very heart and soul into, I began to see it in a different light—which made the process easier and more delightful. It became clear to me that the recipients of what I let go benefit as much or more from my "detachment" as I do. Not only am I moving stagnant energy which isn't useful to me, I am opening the door for someone else to acquire something valuable to them that may not have been possible otherwise. This creates a "feel good" energy, a healing energy—a win-win situation for all parties; sending ripples around the world that will bring rewards in ways not yet imagined. The law of circulation in motion.

Detachment is not just a one-time exercise, it is an on-going process. When my energy begins to feel less than vibrant, or when my creativity begins to feel stagnant, or when my physical space begins to feel crowded, I remind myself of Day 10 and know it's time to exercise my "throwing away muscles" and detach, once again.

Whenever I exercise this very important principle, I am rewarded in ways that I couldn't have predicted. If you haven't taken the time to "detach" do it now—you will be surprised by the results.

— *Vicki Lynn Thull, Vicki Lynn Spirit Art, Racine, Wisconsin*

Dear Dr. Rick,

I am a teacher, a fitness coach, nutritional counselor, speaker, musician and a perfectionist at heart ... or so I thought. So what does this have to do with de-cluttering my house? And detaching from things?

Well ... I was once asked by my life coach, who would you be if you took all those things away? I didn't know where to start because in my mind, that is who I am. The question bugs me to this day, but it is also what gives me inspiration to live with purpose.

So with the utmost ambition to answer this question, I started to unpeel my layers. "Unpeeling your layers" is something you will do for the rest of your life. There is no quick fix, it's always a journey that keeps getting better and better the more you practice it. That is why it is called "practice" so you can get good at it ... just like working out or eating right.

I started detaching from "stuff" around me because that is what I could handle. Day 10 really helped me dig deeper in finding out more about myself than I ever thought I could. I got my boyfriend involved in the detachment process and we started clearing out old clothes to give to Purple Heart and was amazed at how much more space was created! I was thrilled and so was my boyfriend. I couldn't believe how much crowded space really drains your energy. We did this with the kitchen, vitamins, bathrooms, cars, basement, garage, and I really looked forward to it. It became our time away from noise. Getting rid of "stuff" allowed us to focus less on "stuff" and more on each other, our families, and traveling ... which allowed us to live with joy and peace and spread that to other people we interact with.

After I started writing this story, I didn't realize what an impact this exercise had on my life. But it is now a way of life, clear, uncluttered, and beaming with energy because it's not being sucked out of me by stuff, and I'm not defined by what I do or what I know. I am defined by how I love others and my ability to share that through example.

If you choose, ask yourself this question, "Who would you be if you took all of your kids, job, passions, hobbies, and things away?"

It's a great place to start digging ...

Always growing,

— *Shannon Carney, Squeeze Studio Fitness, Brookfield, Wisconsin*

Dear Dr. Rick,

I had an experience recently that *so* reminded me of the day in your program that is about detaching from material stuff and just had to tell you about it.

A friend of mine recently sold her house, and I helped her pack up to move. During this process, she went through a lot of emotions which ultimately led her to the most empowering truth. It all started with a simple garage sale ...

She enlisted some help to put on a garage sale to prune out a lot of excess furniture and material stuff that clearly wouldn't fit in wherever she would live next, but she hadn't yet found that place. Well, it got a little complicated, and ultimately the closing got moved up and she had to abandon the "sale" idea altogether.

She still had major furniture left and made a radical decision about it. She *gave* it away! She found surprisingly that it made her really happy to do it.

It was all that stuck energy about so much stuff that she was feeling crushed by; and once she gave all that furniture away, she felt absolutely elated and free. And she was amazed by those feelings, and that she actually did it. She was overcome with happiness because of the feeling of freedom she was having, and she didn't give a rip about not getting any money for it—it no longer mattered to her!

She is still, weeks later, absolutely reveling in how wonderful she feels because she feels completely unencumbered by *stuff*. Her feeling of freedom is the only thing that matters, and gosh, does it ever matter a lot!

— *Janice, Holland, Michigan*

Hi Dr. Rick,

I've been working on this for more than "Day 10." I always had a tough time getting rid of things, especially paperwork. I "might need it some day" was the mantra.

Recently, I went through some big personal challenges and moved. I was amazed at what I had accumulated after so many years. When I started going through the boxes, initially, it was difficult. I have a keen memory for people and events, so each piece of paper was reliving history. Because my move-out date was coming up, I realized I didn't need to live in the past. I asked myself, "Why was I hanging on to all this old stuff?" Because that's what it was, stuff. And I was starting over.

I started looking at things in a new way. I asked myself, "Did I really need to move all of this paperwork, clothes, etc. to my new, clean space?" and "Where would I put it?" and "Why would I do it?"

It was truly liberating. I donated lots of things, put some things on consignment, and threw out or burned many unneeded things (like paperwork). I now have a regular donation box where I put something in to donate every week, sometimes every day. At the end of the week, I bring the box to a local charity. I have one space where I put items I want to sell on consignment and it's getting smaller.

In your book, you state that detachment makes room for limitless possibilities. I'm ready and open to new possibilities.
— *Wendy J. Terwelp, Opportunity Knocks, Mequon, Wisconsin*

Less is more: Every time you lose some thing, you gain more of you.
— *R.S.*

Day 11

Anonymous Charity:
Buy a Meal

Charity and giving are essential components to happiness. Stretching it even further to anonymous charity will elevate the feeling of joy to a greater level. When an anonymous gift is given, the recipient embraces an awareness that they are being seen, and that they are not alone. Upon acceptance of the gift, they may be inspired to pass it on to someone else in some way. However, the most significant gift is to you, the giver. The feeling of bringing joy to a "stranger" who has absolutely no expectation of this gift, is nearly indescribable. It can only be known through experiencing it, and it can bring about a permanent shift in you: a new way of knowing joyfulness.

Pick a restaurant that you like to go to, preferably with friends, family, or coworkers. The next time you are there, as you are finishing your meal, look around and choose one table to anonymously pay for their meal. Let your instinct be your guide. Perhaps a father with his children, a woman with her elderly mother, or a senior eating alone will catch your eye. The only criterion is that they will finish their meal after you leave the restaurant. After you have chosen your table, contact your server and let them know that you wish to keep this act anonymous. Ask the server to quietly get their bill and put it on your tab, including the tip. If you are with your kids, it is fun to let them participate in the choosing of the table. They will feel charity in it as well.

The impact you will have in this Action Step is many fold. Naturally, you will no doubt feel good about your participation in anonymous charity. The server will experience the positive energy of witnessing a random act of kindness. The people you are with will be curious, even skeptical at first, but they will witness this generosity as well.

If you repeat this act every time you are at this restaurant, there will be another very dramatic impact that you may not recognize right away. The people who are with you, especially your children, will start to consider anonymous generosity to be normal and expected behavior. If there is a first-time guest with you, when you ask your kids to help choose another table to treat near the end of the meal, the guest will be curious and ask about it. Let your kids explain. You will likely be surprised as they explain that this is just something normal that they always do. How wonderful does that sound? Kids teaching that it is normal to give anonymous charity.

If you can, continue the tradition every time you go to that restaurant. You will feel a bit of a buzz from the wait staff and management when they see you. By this effect, you can even elevate the energy in the entire establishment. You will leave a legacy of giving to all involved: the people in your party, the recipients, and the staff at the restaurant. They will all either be inspired to repeat the behavior for themselves, or, at the very least, re-tell the story of the patron who delighted in anonymous generosity. Plan to do this one night this week.

Plant trees in whose shade you may never sit.

Inspired Personal Stories: Day 11

Hi Rick,

Most of us have preconditioned beliefs about money and the judgments we place on money. In fact, money allows you to give back, to support others, and to create positive change in the world. Financial abundance brings your promptings into focus and allows you to act on those promptings in life-changing ways. Today you might act on a prompting by sending a greeting card to someone. A few years from now you may start a foundation as a result of acting on a prompting.

My dad made an impression on me as a young man. He always carried a money clip with several hundreds of dollars in cash, which allowed him to help people in need. Almost every time we ate out as a family, I saw my dad pay for someone else's meal.

When my brother died, my dad's company was going through a rough time. At the funeral, one of his friends gave my dad an envelope. After the service my dad opened it and found enough money to pay for the service. Now, in a time of need, someone showed up to help him. As the saying goes, what you send out is what you get back. After hearing this story, I vowed I would be one of those guys showing up with an envelope.

— *Kody Bateman, founder and CEO, SendOutCards, author of* Promptings: Your Inner Guide to Making a Difference

I decided to add a story of my own here, because a wonderful thing happened to me recently. My daughter Kate and I stopped at a neighborhood restaurant where I first started practicing this lesson years ago. We hadn't been there much recently because I moved across town to be near Lake Michigan.

We happened to get our favorite server of old, Charles. He has absolutely incredible positive emotion and boundless energy. I rose to go to the cashier to ask for my check, when Charles stopped me and said, "someone has already paid your bill, and I can't tell you who it is. The legacy continues." He wouldn't say another word. It's a sweet thought imagining all the possibilities. The laws of the universe are in perfect order. What you send out is what you receive.

— R.S.

Day 12

Productivity II:
Avoid Interruptions

This is the second lesson on productivity. Remember from Day 4 and creating "The Five Things List" that increased productivity will bring increased self-esteem, self-worth, self-love, and joy. Now *that* is what we are working toward together: more *joy* in our lives! That leads us to the second Action Step for productivity, which when combined with the tactic from Day 4, will absolutely make your productivity skyrocket. Believe me, if you can do these two exercises consistently, you will be amazed at the results! So here goes ...

It will not surprise you from what we have learned thus far that the most life-changing exercise can be incredibly simple. So today, I challenge you to choose to *not* check voicemail or email until noon. That's it: don't check your voicemail or email (except the email from me, ha-ha) until noon each day. How simple is that?! It is absolutely amazing how well this tiny shift works. It will allow you to control your focus, put your attention on what is truly valuable and significant to you each day, and help you get so, so, so, so much done. You will find that you can get two days worth of work done by noon each day simply by controlling interruptions.

Timothy Ferriss has some great ideas on training those around you to respect, and ultimately embrace your inaccessibility. He suggests in his best-selling book *The 4-Hour Workweek* putting a voicemail message on your phone line similar to this:

I am currently checking email twice daily, at noon and 4 p.m. If you require assistance with a truly urgent matter that cannot wait until those times, call my cell phone. Otherwise, leave your message and your email address as well, as I am often able to respond faster that way. Thank you for understanding. This move is helping me be more efficient and effective, and to ultimately better serve you!

He writes that if you answer a cell phone call, to let the caller know you are in the middle of something but will take a moment to help them. Keep training and training and training your clients, customers, and any time-wasters to use email instead of over the phone.

Ferris recommends that you turn off any automatic send/receive functions and any distracting audible alerts in your email program. He also suggests putting a similar auto-response in your e-mail program that lets people know the following:

Due to a high workload, I will only be checking email at noon and 4 p.m. This move is helping me be more efficient and effective, and to ultimately better serve you!

These simple adaptations will effectively allow you to avoid two of the greatest interruptions in the modern world!

Now your task is to *do* this. Really, really do it! Record the message on your mobile phone right now! Implement it and avoid the temptation to check those messages. It will definitely take a few days to beat the impulse to be constantly wired and connected, almost like in an addiction, but you will eventually feel comfortable with the peacefulness of not being drawn to the messages. You will reclaim the power and right to control your own time rather than letting yourself and your focus be at the whim of outside demands for your attention. Again, just trust me and do it! Your work time will be filled with the lightness of joy and freedom within a matter of days!

For further inspiration from Timothy Ferriss, read "Chapter 7: Interrupting Interruption and the Art of Refusal" in his book, *The 4-Hour Workweek*. This book was an incredible help to me being more productive, as well as clarifying what I wanted my career to look like and feel like. I invite you to enjoy the liberation of your new productivity!

Gift yourself the freedom to choose WHEN to say "Yes."
— R.S.

Inspired Personal Stories: Day 12

Hi Rick,

I have always been big on productivity. I have always dabbled with trying to protect myself from too much email and voicemail interruptions, but hadn't really committed to consistent behavior around this. So after going through Day 12, I committed to doing that. I started with the weekends, and put my phone in a place that I normally wouldn't see it without a special effort. I wouldn't be prompted to be curious as to missed calls, emails, and text messages

I started to go for hours, and sometimes I would go the whole weekend without even looking at it. When I added this behavior, and really started to do it consistently, I recognized I was actually happier. I also noticed I could really focus my time and it was really liberating. I get real tense sometimes when I'm around my phone and I believe that's because I associate my phone with work and deadlines.

And I think that that's just one of the things that's hurting people in general in society—we're so connected and we're so dialed in every second of every day, I think people have forgotten how to just live a normal life. I think about my parents and my grandparents, and how if they got a phone call a day that was probably a really big event. And obviously there was no email and no text messaging, so how did they communicate? By letter, by dropping over to the neighbor's house, going down to the coffee shop, whatever the case is, and it sounds so simple, but to me—I love it.

So to talk about it from a work standpoint, now that I have trained myself to be able to effectively be away from the phone on weekends, when I really have to dive into a project, I turn my phone on silent and I turn it upside-down so that I can't even see the screen light up, and then I shut down any email programs that I have and I say to myself, "all right self, you're going to get this done without any distraction at all."

The biggest impact for me is not that I can't handle the time management of responding to a couple of quick emails, but it's more about losing that momentum of being really focused and having my mind in the right place to get the highest quality content to come out of me. When I am interrupted, I sometimes find that special creative place I was in can't be recreated.

And if I get that once in a lifetime moment, that idea that just is flowing, and I stop it, I may not ever get it back. That could be a huge loss for me.

So from a personal and professional productivity standpoint and just getting totally dialed in, and making sure that I stay uninterrupted, it really has been life-changing. It's made things easier and better. I have less stress, more happiness, and the feeling of accomplishment that just feels great.

— *Susan Wolff, Arlington Heights, Illinois*

Day 13

Self-Love II:
Admire a Body Part

Today is the day you start loving every inch of you. As always, you know that we cannot give away what we don't possess. In our quest to love others completely and unconditionally, we need to take the first essential step of offering that same unconditional love to ourselves.

You have already picked out a picture of yourself from childhood (Day 6, Self-Love: Your Childhood Picture) that shows you really happy, and you are practicing wishing complete joy and happiness in life for that child. You are continuing to focus on the fact that you are worthy of that unconditional acceptance. To further develop this idea, on Day 7, Finding New Love: Personal Attributes List, you had a Rampage of Appreciation for many of your wonderful qualities, and were encouraged to identify one positive personal attribute each day.

Today the focus expands to loving your physical body, right now, exactly as it is! Begin by singling out your favorite part of your body. It could be your hands, your eyes, your hair, your ankles, the curve of your forearm, the little dimple when you smile, or the laugh lines on your face. Gosh, it could even be your pancreas or your kidneys, which serve you so well every day. It can be anything. Choose this one specific part of your body to accept, appreciate, admire, and love; exactly as it is. Continue all day with your focus on appreciating that one single body part. Think of all the ways you love it, and shower it with admiration.

Tomorrow, choose another body part on which to focus your admiration. The next day pick another, and the next day, another. Eventually you will fall madly in love with all of the aspects of your physical body. Your new and growing self-love will allow you to naturally be comfortable with allowing others to love you exactly as you are. And only then will you be able to extend that unconditional love to others as well.

Speak to no one of what displeases you, not even yourself.
— R.S.

Inspired Personal Stories: Day 13

Dear Rick,

I really believed Day 13 was out of reach for me when I first read it. I felt I was doing well with all the other lessons so far, so I didn't make a big deal about not really being able to write positive things about my physical body.

But then something very unusual came into my life. My best friend's son died in a truck accident, and I spent hours putting a family slide show together showing the joy in his life. Susan, my friend, to show her appreciation, booked us for a pedicure. I had never had one. Because it was gifted to me from a state of pure appreciation for our friendship and the support I gave, the "pampering" felt different. Suddenly I understood what it was to appreciate and love our physical body. As my best friend and I sat in the heated massage chairs, our feet in the wonderful whirlpool, I understood what it was to be a pampered woman, and I experienced bliss. So now I am sharing with you my favorite body part: my pampered toes! I walked out of the salon like I was walking on air!

Thank you for helping me to see what great feelings and love can come from loving a body part. Now that I have broken through with that feeling for my toes, I believe I can expand that feeling of love and appreciation to other parts of my body. Thank you.

— *Carol Newman, Mt. Holly, New Jersey*

Day 14

Wealth Consciousness:
A Check from the Universe

How do we start the flow of more abundance into our lives? As with anything, we start the entry of something into our lives by creating a pathway for it to flow, and then allowing it in. Here is a great Action Step to get that concept started in your finances: write yourself a check!

Get out your checkbook and be creative. Start by making the check out to yourself. Pick an amount that really is meaningful for you, and use the memo section for the specifics of where it is coming from, or what it is intended for. Have fun with it! Perhaps it can be the salary that you want from your next career, or the income you desire from your own business. Or you can choose to make the memo refer to money for a new TV, a new car, or your child's college education. Write about whatever it is that you want to flow into your life.

Now, tear out that check and display it in a prominent place so that you can use it as a visualization tool. Tape it to the mirror in your bathroom, put it on the refrigerator, or carry it in your wallet so that you see it often. What you put your attention on regularly will find a way to show up in your life, so put that check where it will remind you to expect that abundance!

Let yourself be free and creative in your visualization of abundance! No dollar amount or idea is too far-fetched for you. Why not get out your checkbook and make a $50,000 deposit?! Continue to carry the balance forward, writing the number over and over. It's a great way to visualize having enough money for whatever you could possibly want. Become comfortable with expecting that abundance in your life, and open up that pathway for it to flow in!

A lack of money is never a problem, it is only a symptom.
— T. Harv Ecker

I wrote a check to myself for $10,000,000 for "acting services rendered" and carried it in my wallet until it was shredded with wear. it was only a few years until I was able to ask for twice that!
—*Jim Carrey, actor*

We have received hundreds of stories from people who have brought huge sums of money to themselves using "the secret" check. It's a fun game that works!
—*Rhonda Byrne, author of* The Secret

Inspired Personal Stories: Day 14

Hi Rick,

This seemed a bit silly to me, but I did it. I wrote a check to myself for a million bucks. The reason I did a million dollars was because in the memo section of the check, I put down "Colorado Mountain Home." And I'll tell you this: when I see those three words, first it brings a huge smile to my face, but second, it brings back some of those special thoughts and moments that I've experienced as I've really changed my life over the past number of years because it has been such a special place to me.

What's most interesting to me is that now that I have the check, buying the Colorado Mountain Home is not the challenge. The challenge is clearing my life of complications so that I can focus on something that will be even more special, not only to myself and my fiancee and my dog, but for my friends and family to come and experience with me, too.

So it's funny how you have this thing, the check, and you put it in a place that you do see it on a regular basis as a constant reminder that you want it, and you want it for really really great reasons. Also that there's a way to get it, and you just have to be paying attention every day for the things that present themselves that will allow you to experience that lifestyle.

It's amazing where it puts you—those three little words—I don't even look at the dollars anymore, I just look at the three words: Colorado Mountain Home, and I feel like I'm snowboarding every day. It's really incredible.

It just feels perfect, like, you know what? This is it! I'm going out to Colorado and I'm going to start searching for a house, and it's just the right moment. The moment hasn't come to me yet, but I know it will at exactly the right time that this should be in my life, where it's not going to be a distraction, but it's going to be an addition, a really good addition. It's going to be really special.

It is really nice to remind myself by looking at the check that the Colorado Mountain Home is on it's way to me.

— *Alexander, Rockford, Illinois*

Day 15

Consistency of Thought: Cover Your Ears

As you progress through this program and bring more and more positive energy into your life, your consciousness is beginning to transform. You are intentionally creating your own positive personal reality. Some of the people around you may not be ready for you to make these shifts. Have you encountered any resistance to your changes? There are logical reasons why the people you care about may react defensively toward your new and unfamiliar approach to thought. They may feel left behind. They may feel fear or jealousy. This is not unexpected. Try to be at peace with the reactions that come your way, knowing that this adjustment is inevitably part of your significant progress.

To help avoid the discouragement of this initial resistance, it is best to keep many of your new focused desires and your dreams private. Ultimately, you will not be affected by the judgment of others, but early on in the process of change, your new self is vulnerable and it may hurt deeply to hear the criticism of others. For this reason, it is best to initially keep some of your goals and your thoughts private.

My best recommendation is to never get into a conversation

or confrontation where you find yourself on defense. If you are in a place of trying to justify or defend your position, you are in the world of ego, and you cannot manifest in your positive personal reality from that frame of mind. Do not make anyone else's perspective right or wrong. Try to offer acceptance to every opinion, but in turn expect and attract acceptance of your path.

If you find that you are engaged in receiving criticism, it is time to simply "cover your ears." Block it out. Deepak Chopra tells a story of a great wise person who, in their enlightenment, was immune to criticism by others. The wise person's perspective was this: "If someone offers you a gift, and you do not accept that gift, to whom does the gift belong?" Consider this question in relation to the negative feedback that others offer you, and realize that you are empowered to decide whether to accept that negativity or leave it with its giver.

In the face of criticism, simply choose not to internalize or accept it. Never engage in justifying or defending your perspective. The only opinion you need to internalize and develop is your own.

Let your own voice be all that you hear,
When the world tells you "No," cover your ears.
— Randi Driscoll

Inspired Personal Stories: Day 15

Hi Rick,

I relate pretty strongly to the lesson that addresses receiving criticism for your own personal transformation. Raised in a suburban Christian mega church, I have been passionate about my faith for many years and was initially met with much encouragement from those around me. Many of my friends and family consider themselves Christians, so my early ideology of the gospel as call to evangelism was warmly received. However, throughout my college years, as I studied community education and experienced the reality of the inner city, God began to teach me more about a gospel that demands compassion, self-sacrifice … a universal extension of grace and unity of all people, and a life that reflects that work on earth. This journey led me to spend six months in Latin America and on the U.S.-Mexico border, studying immigration firsthand by asking questions of those most profoundly affected by the current lack of reform.

Now that I have returned for a season to the suburb where I grew up, I am disillusioned by the lack of enthusiasm I now receive from those who originally were supportive of my faith. I have found out that even my own tradition, which I had perceived as being open to transformation from Christ's teachings and the guidance of the Holy Spirit, expresses strong resistance to this "less-American" gospel that breaks from political alliance and values the human over the economic. My path has reached some new conclusions that don't fit the pattern I was given to follow.

I am still committed to struggling through many of those relationships—I am not ready to "cover my ears" and completely disengage. I believe transformation and healing through those difficult conversations is possible. However, I agree completely that it is important to create space for yourself to tune out resistance and discouragement in order to continue on your genuine path of growth—the one that stems from your own quiet intuition. I am still learning the art of this balance—how to trust myself admist voices that discredit or argue what I know. But I am encouraged that such opposition is a universally common experience of thinkers and believers that have interpreted the

world in a new and unique way. I am comforted to know I am in good company!
— *Kate Schaefer, recent college graduate, Milwaukee, Wisconsin*

Day 16

Owning Your Thought Sphere: Quiet the Noise

We have been speaking a lot about bringing in more positive thoughts, adding positive images, and staying immersed in positive energy. This lesson is about allowing space for this new positivity by avoiding the negative energy in our environment.

The first thing we will address is the energy of the media. Today's exercise is simple: turn off the TV news, stop watching TV commercials, and no longer look at the newspaper. This is much easier than you think. The evening and morning TV news shows are probably the worst offenders with destructive energy. They thrive on the negative, the tragedies, and the controversial. It also is a very vulnerable time of day for your thoughts: right when you wake, and just before you go to sleep. These are times that you specifically want to create the perfect positive environment for your thoughts to rest in.

Does letting go of the popular news media make you anxious that you simply won't know what is going on in the world? Don't worry: I have found that the big stories always find us somehow if we need to know about them. Are you concerned you are shirking your responsibility to the world?

Think about it: how much are you impacting world events now? Besides, there are hundreds of acts of love in the world for every one publicized act of violence. Those acts of love just rarely make the news.

Don't watch the commercials. They are filled with messages of lack and of fear. Commercials are trying to create a need in you, so that you buy their product to fill that artificial need. The best way to avoid commercials is to never watch live TV. Record anything you think you might want to watch, watch it later, and fast forward through the commercials. Start this tonight by setting the VCR, DVR, or TiVo to record the next show you might like to watch.

You will find that as you do this you will spend less time thinking about and discussing the negative things going on in the world. You will also find that people who feed on negative energy will drift away from you, and go whine about the world to someone else. That gives you more time to allow people who thrive on the positive to find you. That is the Law of Attraction. You don't even need to tell anyone you are making a change or that you won't enter into a negative, whiny, or complaining conversation. You can simply show no interest, and better yet, change the topic of conversation.

Here's an added bonus. Avoiding negative media is also a great time saver, easily giving you more than enough time to do the simple daily exercises I recommend in this Makeover. Let's clear away the negative to make room for the new positive together!

Allow the outside world in only on YOUR schedule.
— R.S.

Inspired Personal Stories: Day 16

Hey,

You are the media operations director for your own life, and you can totally control what information comes into your brain, and what thoughts will be created over and over. Attention to this one thing can completely transform your life!

— *Randy Gage, International Author, Consultant, and Trainer*

You are right, Rick—

Commercials really *are* annoying! I've never watched a commercial and walked away a better person. It's just not good for the way you think. Drug commercials in particular list all the horrible things that could happen to you from taking or not taking something. And much of the time, commercials inform you about things you never even realized were wrong with you. They may send you the message that your cholesterol is high, for example. There is an endless list of things that could be wrong with you that you would never even know about.

And the funny thing is, they are actually creating the symptoms for people because people sit around going "Oh, yeah, holy cow, that might be *me!*" And it's all for marketing. I am so glad that DVR was invented so I can focus on my life and not be duped into the negativity and fear messages of commercials.

— *Doug Frye, Kenosha, Wisconsin*

Hey Rick,

I just discovered the "mute" button on my TV remote. I can't believe it. It was sitting there in front of me all the time. At your suggestion from Day 16, I starting hitting mute at the commercials when my girlfriend and I watch TV. Wow, it's amazing. We talk! It has really helped our relationship.

I have something to add. When I hit mute, I turn to face my girlfriend and she does the same, that way we really get into our conversation by keeping our eyes from the distraction of the TV picture. We notice now that many times we get lost in conversation and don't even notice when our show comes back on. And you know what, we don't even feel as though we are missing anything ... we are actually better for not watching it.

Well, it's been quite an amazing discovery, and I can feel the desire building in me to perhaps not even turn the tube on at all.

— *Leslie, Oshkosh, Wisconsin*

Day 17

Humanism Over Nationalism: Buy a Mug

An everyday reminder, however simple, can assist in shifting our thinking on a significant level. Our focus today is on inclusive positive thinking.

Today's Action Step may be the simplest in the course, but it may also have one of the most lasting effects. Your assignment today is to buy a new mug. Choose one with a message that is purely positive for you, something that is uplifting or playful toward the other beings on the planet. Shop today so you can return home with the mug. If you would like one of our Bless Humanity mugs, visit the Resource page on the home page at www.rickschaefermd.com. When you find the mug that's right for you, purchase it. This will be a small investment with great positive returns. When the new mug arrives home, remove some of the older mugs from the cabinet, and make the new one a favorite, so that you are reminded continuously of the message it holds.

Use this exercise as a starting point to trade nationalism for humanism. The phrase "God Bless Humanity" has impacted my life tremendously in making this shift. Trade the idea of asking God to bless a nation to asking God to bless all of humanity. Trade in your political affiliations for being a card-carrying member of the human race. Look for things that you have in common with all the other people on the planet. For example, you breathe air, your fingernails grow, you like a bit of sunshine, you love family, etc. Look for similarities between people, religions, and cultures. Look for the connections we all have. Identify what holds us all together, and how necessary each of us is for the thriving of our planet.

This new mug, as simple as it sounds, will help remind you of this new way of inclusive thinking. Happy sipping!

Treat others, all others, without exception, as YOU wish to be treated.
— R.S.

Inspired Personal Stories: Day 17

Hi Rick,

I have a mug story for you:

I walked into a Starbucks a few months ago, and noticed that they had some new mug designs on their shelves of cool stuff to buy, and was immediately drawn to the message on one of them. They were promoting the concept of recycling and going green, and so they had a mug that had the word "reincarnate" on it.

I was really drawn to it, because I could feel the feeling of renewal, of new life, and it was inspiring to me to feel that. After leaving the shop, I couldn't get the feeling and the draw to the mug to go away, so I went back and purchased it.

It was a great feeling to gift that to myself. Now, when I use that mug for my morning coffee, it brings me that sense of renewal all over again. I love it! And it fits right in with my other mugs. There's a couple that my kids made for me, with pictures they drew and messages they wrote—I'm always a sucker for them telling me "I love you Mom." I have a "Life is Good" mug, and a "Bless Humanity" one.

It's really cool for me every morning to look at my mugs and choose the inspired feeling that I want to start my day with. It's my morning ritual and I love it. Sometimes, in the evening I'm thinking about the next morning and the feeling, and I want to go to sleep just so that it'll be morning soon! It's really fun for me and I love the way it all feels!

What better way to start the day than with choosing a good feeling and a thought that *life is good!* So anyway, I wanted you to know that the "mug" idea really works for me.

— *JoAnn Monroe, Oak Brook, Illinois*

Dear Dr. Rick—

The recent World Cup competition caused me to think about what you say about "humanism over nationalism," and how nationalism showed up so strongly in the events of the tournament.

This all came up for me when I was chatting with someone I know who lives in Barcelona, as he was describing the celebrations that went on because of Spain's victory over all of the other competing nations.

Your idea of focusing on the love aspects in regard to other people and nations inspired in me the idea of applying the concept of love as power in replacing the normal view of competition being about "beating" someone else.

I realized that using love as the powering thought and energy really can apply in competition, although that might sound kind of silly, or soft. And yet, I believe that there *is* a way that is very strong. My idea uses the self-love concept that you promote about loving our physical bodies. It seems like athletes are perfect for this practice just because they are so in touch with their physical selves.

It's the simple practice of appreciating what their physical body can, and does do, while competing. Putting focus on the amazing things it can do—the muscles performing with great strength, the perfection of the body parts moving together, the senses all flowing together, the hand-eye coordination in sync, the lungs reaching for needed oxygen. The body's ability to step up when asked to do so ... you get the idea. It's all about exploding into the experience of the gloriousness of the abilities and performance of the physical body and reveling in that.

This was my idea of how competitors can not only step out of any of the negative aspects of competition like beating the opponent, but actually become better athletes by immersing themselves in appreciation for their physical bodies. It seems like the possibilities for nationalism to turn in humanism would increase greatly!

— *Jonathan, La Crosse, Wisconsin*

Day 18

Possibilities:
Your Last $5

The amount of abundance or lack in our lives is based completely on perception. In shifting our beliefs and thought patterns about abundance, we are literally creating it in our lives. This is an exercise to help you shift your thoughts from lack to abundance. Whenever you get down to $5 or less in your wallet, simply give it all away. Having less than $5 in your wallet is a natural trigger for thoughts of "I better be careful because the supply of money in my life is really limited." This pattern of thinking is coupled with anxiety and holding on too tightly to what we do have. However, if you learn to shift your thinking, having nothing in your wallet can inspire all sorts of thoughts: not of lack, but of abundance. You can create the feeling of opening up all the possibilities in the world. Open yourself up to the place of trust and the mystery of "Where will my abundance come from?"

What comes back will likely be much greater than what you give away. Through giving away your last $5, you will learn the trust associated with true generosity and freedom from the compulsory need for material things to provide security in your life. In this new freedom, you may be rewarded and find money on the sidewalk, get an unexpected check in the mail, get an unexplained deposit to your checking account, or get an offer to go to lunch with a friend.

As a way to help you get a feel for this, and set the habit in place, empty your wallet right now. Experiment with the feeling, and see where it leads you. It may simply lead you right to the ATM, which is great, too! It still demonstrates that abundance finds you.

The Universe loves to fill a vacuum.

Inspired Personal Stories: Day 18

Dear Dr. Rick,

I had a fun experience on Day 18. I actually spent my last $5.00 on that very day. Later in the day, I went to my online checking and discovered an $18.00 deposit in my account! It was a refund I wasn't expecting.

— *Jack Green, Flossmoor, Illinois*

Dear Dr. Rick,

Let me share something I now do that feels inspired by your Day 18. When I am at a restaurant, I carefully eat my meal leaving exactly one bite of each part of the meal for last, making sure that it is the primest most perfect bite of the whole meal. Then, instead of savoring the last, best bite for myself, I offer it up to another at the table. It's not unusual to share a bite for taste among dinner guests in my contact circle, so this is not the unusual part.

The unusual part is that it is the last bite. It is funny, though, how resistant the recipient may be, knowing it's my last bite. But eventually they succumb to my loving authenticity. The part that makes this so special is that it is the most carefully chosen best bite that becomes my last bite. This is where the magic is. I can feel emotion in me that fills me up over this simple offering.

I believe what it represents is this whole lesson on possibilities. By offering up my last best bite, I am open to the world to provide me my next meal, knowing not where it may come from, understanding the security and infinite possibility that lies within the void of gifting my last bite. It is a symbol to help me feel the abundance of food and nutrition on this Earth, and that I can give up something and trust that more will appear in the future.

I know this sounds a little complicated, but I can tell you the feeling is really big. It goes with that saying you have about the Universe loving to fill a vacuum.

Mmmmm, I can't wait to see what my next first bite will be!

— *Alex Williams, Excelsior, Minnesota*

Day 19

Triggering Positive Energy Unexpectedly: Reprogram Your Ring-Tones

Much of this program is about replacing the existing outside world with your intentionally created inside world. A lot of the energy of that process is directed toward adding in positive signs, signals, and information, and removing negative unwanted stimuli carrying negative or old energy and paradigms. Remove the programming from the past, your "old busted" thinking that is no longer serving you, and replacing it with the "new hotness" thinking, which will take you anywhere your heart desires.

Today's exercise is directed toward removing some old sounds and stimuli and replacing them with new, more beautiful sounds.

Take your cell phone and replace your current ring tones with some of your favorite uplifting songs from your favorite moments in life. Let these be songs that remind you of high school, your first date, your first kiss, your first child, a great vacation ... any of your happiest times. You already know exactly which songs those are, because whenever you hear them, a positive image comes to mind automatically.

You can get these ring tones by ordering them through the Internet on your phone, going to an Internet site from a computer, or using a computer music program to make your own. One way or another, find a way to put beautiful music into your phone (don't be afraid to ask someone to help you if you need assistance in figuring out how—it's another opportunity to share the positivity of this Action Step!) Have fun choosing different songs to represent different people when they call.

After doing this, I have found that sometimes when my phone rings, I enjoy the music so much that I am delayed in answering or even miss the call altogether and have to call back. What is so valuable about this is that it shifts your mindset into a positive, uplifted happy place before you even answer the call. You are jamming along with the music, and sometimes that joy spills over and you just want to share the great song by continuing to sing it to the caller when you pick up.

This technique is especially valuable for calls that you consider a nuisance, whatever that means for you. It could be wrong numbers, creditors, the office, your toughest customer, or even a relative. I have found that for me, the nuisance calls are from "Unknown" callers (or telemarketers), and I have decided to use a soft and spiritual version of "Amazing Grace" for that ring-tone. It is amazing how well it works. I hear this beautiful whisper of "Amazing Grace" in my ear and I know I don't have to answer or even check the phone. It is really nice: instead of being interrupted and having to check the phone and be frustrated with another unknown caller, I just enjoy the song, smile, and let it go to voicemail. Wonderful!

Here's an extra idea: set your cell phone to give you an "appreciation alarm" a couple times during the day with a beautiful tune that you don't use for anything else. Let that sound remind you to consider what you are grateful for in this moment. It is a great technique to easily and quickly transport yourself to a place of appreciation.

Happy listening!

Good, good, good, good vibrations ...
— The Beach Boys

Inspired Personal Stories: Day 19

Rick,

I took your suggestion about reprogramming the ring-tones on my mobile phone—that has been so much fun!! I was very particular about it—for one of my daughters, I chose the section from the song "Butterfly Kisses" that goes "precious love of mine, spread your wings and fly," which brings a very tender feeling to me every time I hear it. For my other daughter, I chose a section from a song that actually uses her name. That brings a very sweet, happy feeling to me each time I hear it. It's so cool! I love it when my phone rings!

— *Vanessa, Oak Creek, Wisconsin*

Day 20

Manifestation: Create a Genie Board

When we put our attention on something, it expands. If we obsess about something, it becomes our reality. Have you ever noticed that sometimes you have to ask for, or think about, what you want more than once? To get cream for your coffee in a restaurant, you might have to ask twice. To get help raking the autumn leaves, you may need to ask your kids five times. To get healthy and in shape, you might need to exercise several times a week. To get into medical school, you might need to have unwavering focus for years in college.

Children are masters of this whole manifestation-by-attention thing. I knew a five-year-old who was relentlessly begging his grandfather to buy him a toy. I playfully asked the child how many times he would have to ask before his grandfather would say "yes." The child answered without hesitation, "fifteen times!" Kids really know how to direct their unwavering attention onto something. It just might be that simple. So now it is time for you to start asking again.

This Action Step is simply about putting out a map with directions for where you are headed. This tool for manifesting is quite well known. It is commonly known as a dream board or a manifestation map. I like to call mine a Genie Board. That is because I have the word Imagine at the top of the board. As you look at the word imagine, break it up, and you start to see I M A GINE, or "I am a genie." And of course, you know what genies do: they grant wishes!

So put up a poster board, or a bulletin board, or use the refrigerator, and start placing images of what you want. Cutting pictures out of magazines really works well. It can be material objects, like a Corvette, or a flat screen Sony, or a new home. It can be words cut from magazines that help you find a feeling, like the word freedom, or love, or peace, or travel. The more nonspecific you are about the details of your request, the more magical the possibilities of what the universe can bring you. You can put images of parts of the world you want to see, images of health and exercise, images of people laughing together, images of kids and parents peacefully sharing a meal, images of lovers holding hands or sharing a kiss. Make sure that you put your Genie Board in a place where you will see it very often!

As in Day 15 Cover your Ears, you really don't want to put yourself in a position to ever have to defend or justify what is on the Genie Board. If people see it, feel free to say, "this is just what I like to do." Don't explain or have a need for them to be supportive, just let them observe you on your journey. Don't give others the power to take positive energy away from your process.

Sometimes this manifestation technique works in really extraordinary ways. In the movie *The Secret,* John Assaraf speaks of cutting out a picture of a beautiful home from a magazine and putting it on his dream board. Over time, his dream board went into storage. However, five years later, when he was unpacking boxes after moving several times and found the original dream board, he realized to his surprise that he had just moved into the actual home in the picture!

So, let's get to work dreaming! Grab some magazines and a scissors, and start cutting out some cool images! But watch out—it really happens much faster that you think. Maybe some of your wishes will begin to manifest even before the glue dries!

Be careful what you wish for ... you just might get it!
Well, duh!!!
— R.S.

Inspired Personal Stories: Day 20

Dear Dr. Rick,

My life was in total shift, because I had just sold my house and given away all of my furniture. I had a one way ticket to Europe. One day I wandered into a furniture store whose unique imported furniture I loved. Then I saw it - an elegant French Provincial, all carved and curved and hand painted and signed by the artist. Creamy white with roses and butterflies, symbols of my growth and freedom. But the price! The armoire, triple dresser, two night stands, head board and carved mirror all added up to $29,000. I had $30,000 left from selling my house. I could stay and have my bedroom, or have my dream adventure and discover the world, and a whole new courageous me. My inner voice told me that this journey was most important and so I simply took photos of the bedroom set of my dreams.

I left on my grand adventure and traveled Europe for 3 years. I often looked at the photos of my dream bedroom set that I kept tucked away and knew that someday I would have it. I always felt confident about it.

When I returned to the United States, I called my friend Julie, who had gotten married while I was overseas. She invited me to her new home. When I walked in, I was rather surprised because I knew that she loved very contemporary furniture, but her home had very ornate furnishings. She explained that just before they married, her husband's mother had passed away and all of this was inherited from her. When I saw her bedroom, I literally squealed because *there was my bedroom set*. Exactly the same one! I told her that if she ever wanted to sell it to please call me. I took more pictures of it and put them on the wall of my bedroom.

One year later Julie called me to offer it to me. My boyfriend Wally was visiting me that weekend. We drove to Julie's but I didn't tell him why. Julie and I talked about a price. She knew I didn't have much extra cash because I was building my new coaching business. She asked for $1,000. I said yes, not knowing where I would get it from. On the way home Wally asked me what that was all about and I told him the story. He said, "let me give that to you for your birthday." I cried and accepted his gift. We picked it up that day, and *my* perfect bedroom set was in my

room that night. Thank you, Universe for my Divine Gift!
— *Sunni Boehme, Life Coach, Bay View, Wisconsin*

Day 20 is something I had worked on once before, several years ago. I remembered having some success with it and was eager to try it again. I recently moved to a new apartment. An unexpected surprise was waiting for me. At the end of my hallway in the new apartment is a large cork board. It is the ultimate "genie board." I have several items there now. As things are manifested, I can pull them off and add something in place of the last item.

I think the most fun thing for me about all this is that I actually manifested the Genie Board itself.
— *Jeanette Geder, Milwaukee, Wisconsin*

Thoughts become things. Choose wisely!
— *Mike Dooley, Author,* **Notes From the Universe**

Day 21

Focus of Thought:
Sit in Silence

The nature of our minds is to be constantly active, racing with tasks and emotions like a hamster on a wheel. And the main problem with this ceaseless chatter is that it is mostly a continual recycling of the same old (and usually busted) thoughts. Once in a while, a new thought or idea pops in, but soon it is back to the same old cycle.

Meditation offers a break from this pattern, offering peacefulness and new possibilities in its place. Just as for an artist a blank canvas offers so many creative possibilities, so is it with your mind. Clearing it will bring a rush of creative energy!

The challenge is to deliberately replace the chaotic jumble of thoughts with just one thought, and then ultimately no thought at all. I believe this takes a bit of practice to achieve, so let's just shoot for the "one thought" goal to begin with.

Sit in a comfortable chair, allowing your body to be relaxed, your weight grounding you in the chair and connecting you to the earth. Close your eyes and slowly take a deep, cleansing breath. Now, focus all of your attention on your breathing; in and out, in and out. When you catch your mind wandering, bring your attention back to your breathing. If it helps, you can think of the 24 second clock in basketball. Watch the numbers tick down toward 0. If your mind wanders, go back to 24 and start again. After five minutes has passed, bring yourself back to noticing your body and your surroundings. Notice how clear and peaceful your mind feels, centered and ready to return to your day.

Don't be discouraged if it is difficult to slow your mind down, or if the opposite happens and you doze off. The process is still really beneficial. It takes practice to break the habit of constant anxious thought, and in the meantime you will benefit from this quiet period by opening up your mind to be more relaxed and gain creative energy.

On a daily basis, make the five-minute commitment to silence. See how dramatic the change is!

Thinking less makes it more effective.
— R.S.

Inspired Personal Stories: Day 21

Dear Rick,

During my journey of evolution, which has been the last ten to twelve years, one thing I have loved doing is meditating. Being able to sit in silence with no outside noises has felt very peaceful and nurturing to me.

I've found that the practice of meditating has been a bit challenging because of the difficulty in quieting my mind and not thinking any thoughts. When I reflect on what the job is that our minds have, which is to think all the time, it makes sense to me that it would be difficult! It's sort of like asking my lungs to stop breathing. Not so easy!

So over time, I tried different tactics like listening to a CD with white noise sounds, or using a visual like a blank TV screen. Those were great experiments and helped some, but my mind still kept racing—or trying to race. As you suggest in Day 21, I found if I thought one simple thought, like following my breath as it came into my body and then left, or repeat one word in my mind over and over, that my mind was happy because it had something to do. As it turns out, having that one thought isn't enough to disturb my meditative state, which is great. It's just enough to allow my mind to be peaceful and do what it needs to, and then it stops bugging me!

Meditating is such an important practice for me to have because it allows me to find peace inside of myself, and feel myself connecting with a greater part of me—the wise part, the calm part, the part that knows that all is well. Those are feelings that I find worth feeling each and every day!

— *Amani, Brookfield, Wisconsin*

Day 22

Parenting with Love:
Display a Wallet Picture

Today's lesson is so simple, and really has a sweet energy about it. It will remind us that each of us possesses a young, sweet, and innocent energy, and oftentimes the example of children, who hold this energy in its purest and most apparent form, are the best reminder for us to treat each other with the kindness and patience that a child deserves. Pick someone that is really dear to you—if you have children, they will work perfectly for this Action Step. I will describe this exercise as if you are using your own children because that is how I've done it, but remember that any child that has a special place in your heart will be just as effective.

Find a picture of your kids when they were at their most innocent and trusting age, happy and playful, and connected to their true selves most completely. Choose ages when they interacted in an irresistible fashion—when they were so into you, thinking you were the most amazing person on earth. Take that picture and pop it into your wallet where you will see it every time you open it. If you do not have that type of wallet, place it in your purse or in some place where it will surprise you every day: inside the fridge, or one of the kitchen cabinets, or next to the speedometer in the car, or on the back of the closet door so you'll see it each morning. Anyway, the wallet idea works so perfectly for me. The picture always surprises me, and oftentimes others see it and ask about my adorable, beautiful, precious kids. In the picture they are probably two, six, and eight years old, and now the older two are off to college! So it's really fun to be asked and to tell their stories.

The reason behind all this is to be reminded of the true energy and spirit that lies within the children. That energy and spirit they hold at their most precious innocent age when they adored you, came running to you whenever you came home, exclaimed "watch me, mommy!" whenever they did something new, when they were never going to stop kissing and hugging you, and snuggling you, and getting tucked in each night, and claiming they would someday live across the street from you. Oh, that precious, adorable age!

The secret is that the energy that lived in them then, still lives in them today. The picture that looks back at you will be a daily reminder of who those children really are, and how they feel about you. It will remind you to treat them in that same way you used to when they were so young and fragile. Despite the more independent exterior that we all develop as we grow, remember that they still want to be loved and admired and nurtured, and especially told that they are the most wonderful children in the whole world.

They are today still holding the energy they held in that picture. They are still madly in love with you! Don't ever forget it!

They are madly in love with you. Always have been, always will be.
— R.S.

Inspired Personal Stories: Day 22

Hi Dr. Rick,

In Spring, I went in to see my high school guidance counselor. I walked into his cramped office. Papers were sprawled out everywhere. He was just getting off the phone. His schedule was always packed, whether it was rushing kids in and out, tryng to squeeze in as many as he could, or talking on the telephone. I sat down and he said, "Hello." He seemed nice, but I had only seen him a few times for routine "check-ups." The only thing he knew about me was my GPA and the fact that I liked business.

Throughout my junior year, he always started off by asking where I wanted to go to college. My response would always be, "I'd like to go to a big and reputable business school, preferably out of state because I'd like to explore and see what other parts of the country have to offer." His response to that was always, "Have you considered Whitewater? (A small in-state division 3 school.) They have a very good business school." Every time I'd shrug it off by saying, "Yeah, but I'd really like to go out of state," attempting to drop the hint that I had no plans of attending Whitewater.

When I walked in this time, he started off differently. He pulled up my chart, looked at my grades and said, "So, last time you said you wanted to go to Whitewater." That really frustrated me. I didn't want to go there, *he* wanted me to go there and put those words in my mouth. Again, I reminded him I'd really like to go to a big school out of state. Next, I told him I wanted to do a work-study program my senior year. Immediately he exclaimed, "Well, kids who do work-study don't get into the kind of schools you're talking about."

That was the final straw for me. I had had enough of his discouragement and telling me what I could and couldn't do. I could see the doubt in his eyes. He had seen a few letters on a piece of paper and assumed what I could accomplish. He didn't know that I had been running an international eBay business for over four years, selling tens of thousands of dollars worth of items to every inhabitable continent on the planet. He didn't know that I was a private contractor mailing out documents for doctors across the country. He didn't know that I had already received college credit for micro and macroeconomics—the only junior in the school to do so. He didn't know who I was, yet he had the audacity to tell me where I was going ... now how does that make any sense?

Man is on a mission to find the ultimate grading scale to compare or judge people: there's the SAT, the ACT, GPA, class rank, degrees, and salary. These all fail to represent the full person. Some things can't be measured, like a person's drive or passion. Nobody else knows what success means to you and nobody else knows what you want to do and where you want to be. When you know something is right deep down in your heart, you need to embrace it and do everything in your power to go out and get it, no matter what others think or say. Anything less would be selling yourself short.

That's why I'm still doing what I love and feel is right for me, and now I am waiting for the acceptance letter to arrive from that big, reputable, out-of-state business school.
— *James Schaefer, high school senior, Brookfield, Wisconsin*

Dr. Rick,

Talk about parenting outside the box ... I have neighbors that I've known for a long time and know them very well. They are fascinating, in that they are different than "normal" people, different in the sense that they follow their own passions and dreams, rather than following any societally dictated behaviors.

What is so remarkable is how they have role modeled as parents. They have a teenage son, Mark, who at age seventeen has worked independently for over four years running his own online business. He has never been an employee—and he intends never to be one! Wow, that is just *so* different from how most people think, and choose. The list of his exceptional behaviors goes on, too: he purchased a new computer with his own money that he had earned himself! When he was only fifteen.

This exceptional young man is also able to recognize how the school system is *not* supporting his vision. For instance, he was required to write a paper for his English class about future vocations. He wrote all about his dreams of business, of being an entrepreneur and deliberately choosing and creating his future. When his teacher returned the paper to him, having read and critiqued it, she only made comments about his grammar and spelling, etc. Negative comments at that. She made no comment whatsoever about his vision, about his uncommon thinking, or gave encouragement of any sort. This simply emphasized what he has known for a long time; and that is, although the education system wasn't going to support him in his uniqueness, he wasn't going to give up. In fact, it inspired him to consider quitting school and getting his G.E.D. on his own! He is already so involved in his passion that he is ready to burst into the world in a much bigger way. Although he decided against dropping out, even now he is *still* thinking and choosing for himself.

How does a person become so clear at such a young age? Well, certainly the first guess would be that he had a parental influence for it. And that is quite true. This young man has highly exceptional parents. They pursue their inner callings, their passion, with great dedication. Even in the face of resistance from others. And second, they have encouraged and supported their three children to do the same. The children are all clear that they will always be supported when they are following their own heart's desire, and passion; and they each have their own, unique interests and calling. The kids know that they can share their passions and desires with their parents, and that they will be supported, even if it is not an endeavor that the parents specifically personally support ... if the kids are passionate about it, the parents will support it. This is amazing role-modeling for the children.

The evidence is clear and undeniable. Going against the flow of common thinking can only open the possibility of being, and living, a unique life. Now that's something to write about in the parenting magazines!
— *Brenda, Sheboygan, Wisconsin*

Dear Dr. Rick,

We have a son who is just really not that interested in academics. He is now going to be a junior in high school, and clearly in middle school, his interest really started to fade, as did his grades. We made the decision after eighth grade to put him in a private school that could really attend to his needs, and really push him to excel academically. In preparation for the private high school, we hired a private tutor and had him work in areas that the new school recommended.

Well, now, two years later in the specialty, expensive, academically focused private school, our son is still just really not that interested in academics. After reading your Day 22, we decided we were really not helping him much by pushing him to focus all his time in areas he is not interested in. We wish for him above all to be happy and secure, and love life.

He has a lot of passions, including baseball and swimming, music, and building with his hands. We realize now we may be off track pushing him to do well in areas of little interest to him. At the same time, we were stealing time away from him to do work in the areas of his greatest interest. In addition, I believe we have been eroding his self-esteem by putting his focus in areas where he does not excel. We have now committed to making this year a year of focus in the areas that truly inspire and motivate our son.

When we got the email from you with the message, "do not ask what the world needs. Ask what makes you come alive. Because what the world needs is more people who have come alive." This is the gift that we wish to give our son: our full support to pursue the areas that inspire him to truly come alive in this world. We are so grateful to have found this truth, and grateful that it did not come too late. Thank you.

— *Steve and Maria, Minneapolis, Minnesota*

Day 23

Imagination:
Create Your Perfect Day

We know that sending out positive energy brings it right back in our direction, so let's focus on creating some of that light and positive energy. Today's exercise is pure fun! It is writing a tale of your most perfect day, as perfect as you can imagine it. You can bring anything into the story that you like. You can be presented with the Nobel Peace Prize, you can win the lottery, you can get a big raise at work, you can find buried treasure in your back yard, you can meet your soul mate, you can kiss in public, you can discover a cure for cancer, you can eat a whole chocolate cake ... the possibilities are endless! As you imagine, feel the feeling of everything going your way.

Fix your attention on the happiness the events in your tale bring you. Engage in a heartfelt conversation with your teenage daughter, find a quarter on the sidewalk, receive a really warm smile from someone on the bus, get a call from your best friend from high school, imagine your boss appreciating you ... just feel darn good all day!

Start your tale of the perfect day from the moment you open your eyes and awaken. Have total fun with it. Write about anything that feels good. Put the focus on people, or stuff, or awards, or health, or relationships, anything at all. Play with it. Be imaginative. Let that energy start flowing. It seems simple enough, but the positive returns will be many fold.

Start writing!

Imagination is everything. It is the preview of life's coming attractions.
— Albert Einstein

Inspired Personal Stories: Day 23

Hi Rick,

I think it's mostly about choice for me. It's looking back and realizing, "Hey, that was the perfect day!" It's waking up on my terms whenever I want to. It's doing whatever I want to do, and enjoy doing, playing a round of golf, or spending the day with the kids, or going to the lake, or coaching a basketball game ... best yet: doing all those things. What I want to do in the moment. It's not being imprisoned by the "shoulds" and the "have tos," but choosing with my friends, spouse, or kids; we went to Disneyland and had many perfect days there.

What I've observed is that it is important to notice when you have one. Sometimes, a few days later, I realize what a perfect day was when I am doing things that I "have to" do, and a few days before I was enjoying choice.

I've always thought about what it would be like to enjoy the perfect day. I now realize how to make it happen. For me it's about choice and noticing when it is happening. I know I'll want another and another.
— *Dr. Chris Milkie, Mayfair Foot Clinic, Wauwatosa, Wisconsin*

Hi Rick,

I went through this lesson over a year ago just on a whim, and I want to let you know what happened. I wrote about snowboarding, Jackson Hole, Wyoming, getting a massage, and meeting up for dinner with the girl of my dreams. Many of those things have come true for me. I have been out to Jackson Hole several times on snowboarding trips. I unexpectedly met the woman of my dreams and we're going to be married next year. We will honeymoon in Jackson Hole because it could really be a special place for us.

I don't think I'd be exagerating if I said I think about it every day. I think of a small piece of heaven on Earth and I get the biggest smile on my face and the feelings that are inside of me are just amazing.

It's funny to me how the writing out your perfect day exercise seemed to actually make it happen. Because you finally took that step to say, "alright, if I could have anything at any time on any day, what would it be?" And, boom, you write it down and all of a sudden you start to figure out how you can actually make that happen in your life. And then again, it goes back to having your mind in that place that says, "I can do it, I can do whatever I want, I can make it happen, I can figure it out."

And now I feel like I need to go back and do this lesson again because I want to see what it looks like now compared to what it was before. I'll bet it'll blow my socks off!

— *Kevin Kowalke, Lead Strategist, The Kowalke Group, Brookfield, Wisconsin*

Day 24

Openness and Learning:
Car Audio

What we choose to put into ourselves is what we have to give to others. What we think about, we bring about. These are truths that we have begun to practice from a few different angles so far in this program. Today we will continue to incorporate reminders of these ideas into our lives in practical ways.

This is a very simple Action Step. Turn off the radio in the car, and play something inspirational. Quiet the sounds of talk radio, of people pushing their negative ideas on you, of advertisers trying to fill you with fear or anxiety and motivate you to buy their product. Take proactive control of the sounds that you will internalize, rather than leaving your thoughts to the mercy of a radio host or DJ. Day 15 recommended covering your ears from all the negative information coming to you from the outside world, so that you can better create a positive inside world that you will find joy in living. This Action Step will help further that cause.

Remove all these sounds from the outside world, and replace them with something from your new internal, creative, visionary world. Very simply, put a deliberately chosen tape or

CD in and listen purposefully. Choose something that will uplift you.

Whenever you can when you are driving with others, leave the CD playing as long as possible, even if just in the background at a quiet level. It will have an impact on those around you, too. They might absorb some of the inspiring positive information, or calming sounds. They might see that your proactive approach to what you listen to is causing you to change, and you can be an example to them of how to control the information that you allow into your ears and your thoughts. It might become a habit for them, too, simply because you modeled it for them.

So, I would like you to do two things today. First, start right now by listening to an audio book the next time you are in the car. If ever you need a break from it and crave music, choose music that will be uplifting to you: happy music that might remind you of great times in your life, like the carefree memories of high school or college, the music you listened to when caring for your first child, the song that was played at your wedding ... the list goes on.

Second, treat yourself to something new today. Go to a bookstore or the library, look through iTunes or audible.com and choose a new audio book. Choose something you haven't heard before, from your favorite author, or perhaps something that simply catches your eye and looks good. I believe that when you allow something to "jump off the shelf at you," you allow divine intervention in to bring you something wonderful that you otherwise may not have sought out. You will really feel anticipation around getting started on this new book in the car right away. You may even want to take the scenic route home just so you can keep listening. Even succumb to the temptation to park and gaze at a beautiful view while you listen.

A wonderful side effect of this Action Step is that normally frustrating situations such as being delayed in traffic or waiting for someone you are picking up have a new benefit: you get more time with your new audio-book. This is just another small, daily, practical way that you can shift a pattern of negative response to a positive growth experience.

Bring on those traffic jams!
— R.S.

Inspired Personal Stories: Day 24

Hi Rick,

I can't tell you enough how wonderful your lesson is for Day 24. Now when I'm driving I only listen to stuff that makes me feel good! I have some really cool stuff on my iPod, like uplifting teachers who also make me laugh (very important to me!); and music that I really love that's either sweet and soft and touches my heart, or such darn good dancing music that I can hardly sit still in my seat! And, can't stop myself from singing out loud! I love it, I look forward to driving, and even have made traffic jams my friend. Who would have thought that would ever happen?!
— *Sara, Paducah, Kentucky*

Hi Rick,

There is one thing that I have done which has impacted me the most in my evolution into more of myself and my natural joy. It has been my spiritual practice of turning my car into my personal wellness center by listening to words of wisdom from the teachers that I respond to most strongly. I listen to CDs and tracks on my iPod, using a random setting and trusting that what comes up is the perfect thing for me to hear to shift my thinking into something lighter, or healing, or joy filled. It works every time.
— *Damian James, Detroit, Michigan*

Day 25

Self-Love III:
Fill Your Own Tank First

This lesson is about keeping your own tank full. You will have nothing to give to others is you don't have it yourself! Be selfish in a positive way.

Being "selfish" is such a loaded concept in our society. We're told by our family from an early age not to be selfish; that selfish is bad, and no one will like us if we are selfish. Well, consider for a moment that the opposite is true. Selfish is good. Actually, it's vital! And isn't it interesting that we are told by others to think of "others" first? Hmmm ... who does that serve?

On an airline, they teach that if the cabin should depressurize and the oxygen masks come down, to always put your mask on first, before you attend to anyone else, even your own child! Isn't it amazing that we have to actually be reminded to take a breath ourselves first?

No one else is responsible for our happiness. Only we are. Once we accept that, take responsibility for it, and embrace it, we are free to explore the limitless ways that we experience happiness and seek them out on a daily basis.

Today, keep a small notepad with you. As you go through your day, notice as many things as you can that bring you a feeling of joy. Is it watching a caterpillar go squirming past you on the sidewalk? Is it getting together with friend? Is it watching the sun go down over the horizon? Is it going for a run early in the morning? Is it taking a class such as yoga, or learning Spanish, or studying for an MBA? Is it baking a cake with your child? Or by yourself? Is it reading in your favorite chair for twenty minutes? Or perhaps sneaking in a ten-minute nap?

Remember, this is a focus on what really makes *you* feel good. Really go deep into these moments and say, "This makes *me* feel good. *Me, me, me!* And making *me* feel good is really great because then I will be better able to give to others, and make *them* feel good too. Mmmm, but *ME* first!"

Do you know how easy it is to give when you feel like you have treated yourself to something special? It makes you want to share that feeling with others. And coming from that point of being really filled up yourself, you will be so much fuller in your giving to others. Gone will be the feelings of obligation or reluctance in being generous and allowing with others. They will really feel your joy, because *you* really feel it!

There is an endless list of things that can delight you. Just jot down anything you notice that makes you feel happy. At the end of the day, take a few minutes to recall how good it felt to experience those things, and remember that you were filling up your own tank. The fun part is that by giving to yourself, you are also better able to give to others. Everybody wins!

Make your most "significant other" yourself.
— R.S.

Inspired Personal Stories: Day 25

Hi Rick,

I was a prosecutor for the Chicago Cook County State's Attorney's Office. I was one of the first women in the felony trial division which handled all the most serious jury trials. To compete with the men, I buried my emotions and lived through my ego. I didn't believe in anything that I could not hold in my hand and show to the judge or jury members. Then, one day while walking my dog Buddy in the forest preserve, I heard a voice that said "why do you hate yourself?" I knew there was no one there but the two of us, and Buddy was not known to be that vocal, nevertheless I "felt" this was something needing a reply.

Not accepting the premise, I began arguing with the voice that I *did* love myself. Back and forth we went, until the voice changed the question to "why don't you like yourself?" That broke through the emotional blockade and every disappointment, frustration, and unfulfilled desire flooded out. Here I had always thought I was happy, and yet I watched my world crumbling around me.

I realized that day there was much more to my journey than the life I was leading. I went in search of the real Toni—the very essence of my soul! The deeper I dug, the more unconditional love I exposed; it had been right there inside of me the whole time. I tore down the remaining walls surrounding my ability to love and to feel both myself and others. Since then, each day has been filled with incredible experiences.

Every day now I talk to that voice which I came to recognize was one of my guides. He has helped me to find the way to live every moment of every day in love. Love of myself, the experience, even the lessons which don't turn out exactly as I would have hoped. I embrace every opportunity presented to me as a step toward my growth and the understanding of life and myself. I will never deny myself those situations again by hiding behind fear.

I have altered my vocabulary to exclude negativity. I begin the day commenting on how fantastic I feel, even if the old bones are creaking a little. The day is bright and shiny even if it has to pass through a bout of cleaning and ironing. The world is at peace even if complaining people have to be dealt with. I create my world, and it is based on love! Come join me.

— *Toni Ann Winninger, J.D., author of* Talking with Leaders of the Past, *Lake Bluff, Illinois*

Day 26

Your Contact Sphere:
Create an Up-Lifters List

It is well established that the people with whom you spend the most time are the people you will eventually be most similar to: in thinking, in habits, in language and, indeed, in income. This Action Step is to examine the nature of those you spend the majority of your time with.

Get out paper and a pen. Make two columns, labeling the left "Up-lifters and Lovers," and label the right "Friends and Others." Now think of the people you most care for in the world, and place their names on the paper. The ones that have purely positive thoughts wrapped around them go on the left. These are the people with whom you feel no controversy—those that you feel total acceptance from.

The people to whom you react with mixed emotion, no matter how close you feel you are to them, or how much you love them, go in the right column. It will be quite revealing to you as you examine the list. There may not be as many people on the left as you might have expected. Now reflect on the amount of time you spend with people on the right. You may be spending a huge amount of time with folks who do not feed you in a purely positive way.

As your consciousness shifts into this new awareness, your circle of friends changes as well. That is expected. No worries. I suggest that you gently shift your emphasis of time and energy toward the people on the "Up-lifters and Lovers" list. You will feel great relief excusing yourself from the obligation of hanging out with the ones in the righthand column quite so much. Over time, as you gently shift attention, perhaps some of the people on the right will change what part of them they show you, and jump over to the list on the left. In addition, many new relationships will be attracted who land on the list of Up-lifters. It is simply the law of attraction at work at its best!

This is not an exercise that is meant to place judgment on anyone else's behavior or habits, so don't allow guilt to weigh you down as you honestly evaluate your relationships. It is simply meant as a tool for you to examine your own contact circle. You have the power to evaluate that circle, and make sure that they continue to feed your mental and spiritual growth. People come in and out of your life all the time—it is a natural consequence of your time on this Earth. Consider old neighbors, grade school teachers, baby-sitters, piano teachers, dance instructors, and your sports coaches. They all have a time and place when their impact and contribution to you can be dramatic, and then they are off to contribute to the journeys of others. And you are left to savor the memory of the effect they had on you.

Because this is not an exercise of judgment or an attempt to change anyone else, it is best if you keep this list to yourself. You actually need not physically keep it at all. Simply the act of writing it will be enough for your expanded awareness and growth toward positive contributors in your life.

Whenever you find yourself on the side of the majority, it is time to rethink your position.
— Anon.

Inspired Personal Stories: Day 26

Hi Rick—

Wow, your lesson on making an Up-lifters list in Day 26 was really big for me, personally, and it also helped me encourage a good friend of mine to set boundaries regarding one of her sisters.

In the past, I have felt confused about what to do with relationships that have controversy in them because I've been taught that we are the point of attraction for everything, and everyone, that shows up in our lives. I've wondered what I am emanating that draws unwanted experiences to me.

Once I made my Up-lifters list, I could really see (feel, actually), who feels purer to me and who doesn't. And it has really freed me to let go of those people whose energy consistently leaves me feeling unsettled. What a relief! Just the giving permission to myself to value the quality of my feelings and energy has been a huge gift!

Meanwhile, I choose to continue to work on being aware of my own thoughts, feelings and energy so that I am shifting inside. I hope that by doing that, I will become an attractor of the up-lifter that is present in all of the people I care about, and whoever comes into my life in the future.

— *Heather, Oconomowoc, Wisconsin*

Dear Dr. Rick,

I was recently at a national event of really amazing entrepreneurs, and I was struggling with feeling that although I had experienced great success, I was hitting a ceiling for some reason and I couldn't break through it. I was very frustrated with where I was at, but then I heard a speaker named Jim Rohn (he has since passed away). Jim was like a modern day philosopher—he was just so eloquent, and something that he said had an amazing impact on me. He said that "you become the average of the five people that you spend the most time with." I didn't immediately let it sink in, but I kept that idea with me. I wrote it down in my daily planner so that I would revisit it daily. I began to look at the people in my life that I spend the most time with, and a few things came into focus.

One thing I realized is that some of the people in my life were totally negative. I noticed that when I was around those people, it caused me to think of all the troubles and problems in life. So I started by making a decision to not have those people in my life anymore. It was a very challenging decision because they were people that were really close to me for a long time, so I had to break some really strong relationships. But I realized that I had to do it to become the best person I could be.

Beyond that, I began to evaluate the business people I spent time with and realized that every one of them was not at my level in terms of business success and income level. As I dug deeper, I was able to realize that it made me feel good when I was in a position where I was compared to them and could play the role of the successful one—the advisor. What I hadn't realized is that it was actually holding me back. So again, I stopped spending time with them and I sought out people who were at levels beyond me.

When I started to do that, it was unbelievable the impact that it had on my mindset, my pocketbook, and my overall happiness. I realized that people who were ahead of me personally and professionally were much happier! They were actually enjoying three-week vacations, lots of time with their families, or whatever they wanted in life. At the time I really wanted to take trips to Colorado, spend weekends in Boston, and not worry about what other people think. And now, the sky's the limit! My new contact circle helps me believe that there's nothing out there, personally or professionally, that I can't achieve. And it's a really nice place to be!

The biggest lesson that I learned is that most people think life's about luck, but it's not. It's about choice. It's what you choose to feed your mind. And the company you choose greatly affects that.
— *Kane, South Bend, Indiana*

Day 27

Love of Humanity:
Speaking Words You Want to Hear

It is affirmed by many religious and spiritual viewpoints that divine energy runs through each of us ... that we are all born from the mind of God ... that we live in God and God lives in us. Therefore it is somewhat universally known that we are all somehow connected to all others in some way.

If indeed we all do share some divine energy somehow, and we are in some way connected, then that means there is some common energy in each of us. That, in turn, leads to the conclusion that in me there is a little of you, and that in you there is a little of me. Certainly, we as humans all share an energy. The same mysterious energy that grows my fingernails grows the nails of any man in China, or the Middle East, or Latin America. All across the planet we share a common intent, to be human, each in our own unique way. And it is through this shared energy that I begin to understand that whatever I give out to someone else, I am giving to myself as well.

Have you ever noticed that when you are having a fun, positive exchange with someone, you feel wonderful? And in the same way when you criticize another or get angry, it doesn't always feel good. Is it possible that as you are criticizing another, through this divine energetic connection you feel its resulting negativity yourself?

The Action Step for today is to focus on that concept just for one day, and to subsequently speak, think and live accordingly. Imagine all the people you speak to today having some common energy with you, actually having traces of your very fibers woven within them. Speak to them in a way that you would love to be spoken to. The way you choose to treat people can be playful, comical, short, concise, wordy, nurturing, and loving. You may even choose to send words to others that are the words you desire to hear yourself.

Think about this common energy, and let its reality become very apparent to you. Perhaps even write down the words you most long to hear, and then speak them to someone. You will be surprised, for in some way, they will be returned. What you send out will inevitably come back!

As the day goes on, be more and more bold. Speak to others and treat others truly as you would like to be treated. Do not worry about reactions and opinions that are beyond your control. Focus only on your growth in understanding for the day.

Near the end of the day, reflect on your experience and imagine the whole world acting in this way. Nobody judging anyone. No criticism. No governments telling other countries what to do, or how to behave. Only appreciation and freedom!

Reflect on the lyrics of John Lennon's revolutionary classic, "Imagine," and let the depth and simplicity of his words settle in and transform your understanding.

It is only when we all choose to recognize this shared energy that "the world will live as one."

No tree has branches so foolish as to fight amongst themselves.
— Ojibwa Indian proverb

Inspired Personal Stories: Day 27

Hi Rick,

You are so right about each of us perceiving and interpreting differently. There are 6.8 billion of us now, each having different experiences, cultures, sets of morals, religious beliefs, languages, dialects, childhood upbringing, education, and basically just different life experiences every day.

Did you know each of us also has different receptors? No one sees color exactly the same as anyone else with our seven million cones per eye. No one hears sounds exactly the same as anyone else with the three thousand cochlear hairs cells in our inner ear. No one tastes, or smells, or feels touch exactly the same with our millions of receptors. And of course, no one has the exact same "sixth sense" as anyone else either.

I totally understand that our differences are what make us strong as a community and as a humanity filling the planet.

— *Jacob, Sun Prairie, Wisconsin*

Hi Rick,

When I was growing up I was around all types of people, racially and religiously. I learned to understand the individuality of others but still realize that the differences weren't enough to have any negative feelings or thoughts about them; I could accept them without question. I have come to appreciate the strength in community that comes with diversity, and differences of opinions.

I have also now come to embrace that some may wish to criticize others, but now instead of trying to get them to appreciate our differences, I think of the "criticizer" as one of the diverse personality types that make my community strong, and simply quietly accept it.

I have found a way to tolerate and appreciate this now. It's a combination of Day 2, Day 15, and Day 27, so I am going to call it the lesson from Day 44! Thanks.

— *Rhona B., Chicago, Illinois*

Day 28

Exercise and Fitness:
Create a Workout List

Our bodies can be physical manifestations that expose our thought patterns and beliefs. Fitness cannot be forced on your body through discipline. Health is achieved only by invitation from the inside. The secret is not to try to change your habits first, but to change your thoughts first. Once your thoughts change, your behavior and your habits will undoubtedly follow, and that will be the key to assured and lasting fitness.

Challenge yourself to embrace the thought that you crave exercise. Use the affirmation "I crave exercise. I can't let the day pass without doing some push-ups and sit-ups. I just go crazy if I don't get my body moving!" These affirmations, although feeling silly at first, will create an inner shift in your thinking; a habit of thought will create a belief, which will in turn result in a change in your behavior.

The Action Step associated with this lesson is really simple, yet can create a massive transformation in your approach to fitness. On a pad of paper write, "I crave exercise, and each day I meet my goal for exercise—often I exceed it!" Under that title make a list in a column: one sit-up, one push-up, one squat, one bend, and one stretch. Each day, check off when you accomplish each task. Keep reading the affirmation on the top of the page when you check off your success. It might seem as if you are setting the goal far too low to have an impact, but it is not the intensity of the physical exercise that we are working on: it is the transformation in your thoughts that is important.

You will create a daily habit of moving and exercising, and you will also be creating an empowered and successful mindset as you achieve your daily goal. You will find that you end up regularly exceeding your goals. And the feeling of success, the feeling of moving toward better fitness, and the true craving of exercise and movement will take root in you so deeply that you will not be able to resist. Your healthy body will be a reflection of your richly healthy thoughts!

Celebrate the small stuff ... and it's all small stuff.
— R.S.

Inspired Personal Stories: Day 28

Dear Dr. Rick,

Your lesson about exercise and fitness has been really wonderful for me, because it helped me immensely improve my thinking about exercising. And, that has helped me feel so much better about it!

A friend of mine and I decided to commit to a regular exercise routine so that we could help each other stay on track with our commitment to exercise daily. We both used to do it consistently, but had found ourselves being very erratic about it and wanted to change that. So we came up with a list of exercises we wanted to do and then created a Google spreadsheet so that we could list them and also track them.

Our spreadsheet was quite complete! We listed the time that we started exercising; we listed the time we ended exercising. Looking back on it now, it was rather hilarious how seriously we took our spreadsheet!

The interesting point of this is that tracking our workouts this way did *nothing* to inspire us to keep going; it felt like a chore, a necessary task to accomplish. *Yuck!*

Then, we used your lesson as our guidance to recreate the feeling of our spreadsheet to something really nice. Instead of logging in times and reps, we entered fun affirmations like "most fun exercising ever!" and "fabulous," and "mmmm, one of the very very best exercise days of my entire life!" Wow, what a difference that has made for us! Now when we think about exercising, we are looking forward to feeling those light, fun feelings—and to thinking up new playful affirmations to enter on our record.

— *Mary, Elm Grove, Wisconsin*

Hi Rick,

I really like Day 28. I truly believe what you say about trusting the body's cravings about food and exercise. Most of us can reflect back on a time when they actually felt "in-shape." You didn't have trouble sleeping. You ate healthy food. You looked good and you felt simply terrific. Once you see yourself as a healthy person who eats sensibly and exercises regularly, your body will take over and practically do the work for you. Our bodies are designed to release powerful, addictive chemicals when we exercise. And the more we exercise the more our bodies will crave healthy food.

I decided to make a choice: to get in the best physical shape of my life. I looked back to when I felt physically the best of my entire life. I then incorporated that thought of feeling physically fantastic into everything I did. My body started craving exercise again and craving really nutritious food.

If I can do it simply by shifting a thought, you can do it, too. Your body will not let you down. Make your own personal decision to be in the best shape of your life. You will not regret it!

— *Tim Schmidt, President, Delta Media LLC, Jackson, Wisconsin*

Day 29

Finding the Perfect Career:
Create a Life Mission Statement

Writing is such a critically important component to manifesting what you want, finding joy, and leading you to Maximum Life! Today we have a writing assignment that can be catered to your own personal writing style. It can be just a bullet point listing or it can be an embellished essay ... depending on where you'd like to go with it.

Today is the day you will write a life mission statement, followed by a career mission statement. You will find that they ultimately are really woven together as one. Simply write down the feeling you want to have about your career and your life, and some of the qualities that must be incorporated in order for this to happen. Focus especially on the qualities that you simply will not compromise on. Perhaps start with the word that best describes your natural role in life: healer, teacher, nurturer, leader, etc. Let the words flow naturally, and be sure to recognize the words that keep coming back. Also look over the writing you did for Day 23's "Perfect Day." This will lead you to incorporate some things you really enjoy.

This Action Step is about connecting with your greatest passion for your life—the reason you are here on this planet at this time and following the voice of your heart. The mission statement will guide you in all of your actions and help you to continually change direction based on the feelings you are having about what you are doing, and how your actions align with your mission.

This is what Rhonda Byrne and all the wonderful coaches and trainers in the movie *The Secret* are talking about. If you can totally commit to what your heart's passion is, and if you have continuing complete focus and drive and passion for this one idea, the universe has no choice but to bow down to you and provide all that you need to complete your goal. Ms. Byrne is a great, great example of that in her creation of the book and the movie detailing this philosophy—everything fell perfectly into place for her because of her complete focus and belief in the project. It was her passion.

Now go write, and continue to rewrite over the days and weeks ahead. Focus and refocus on what you really want. It doesn't matter the vagueness, roughness, or clumsiness of your initial writing. Keep editing and revising, and your statement will eventually describe perfectly what it is that you want.

If you are like me, you will find that you are not always following your mission, and you will have to stop doing some familiar things and start doing some new things. Don't be discouraged—just keep your mission in mind and keep moving towards it!

How will you know when you have it right? By my experience, you can feel it emotionally. How will you know when the details and the vehicle to move closer to carrying out your mission arrive? You will feel it, again, very strongly emotionally. Think of it this way: if you knew you had only six months to live, would you want to do what you are about to do today? If you would, then you already are acting in very close alignment with your mission.

I realized today's lesson for myself when I was half way through creating this program. There is nothing I would rather be doing than completing it. There is nothing that could make me feel more inspired or more alive than working on it, and moving the Extreme Thought Makeover™ one step closer to completion.

So the key to today is just to start writing. Be clumsy and unsure at first and let yourself have fun with it, and eventually your clarity will move you toward living the life that you truly desire!

Become the person you dreamed about becoming when you were a child.
— R.S.

Samples of Life Mission Statements:

My life's vision is in a place that nurtures all life, values integrity and creates financial serenity. It is a place where we honor and celebrate uniqueness, Inspire and empower community, encourage and cultivate acceptance, peace, and love, and live with bliss
— *Teri Williams*

I am a Joy Guide. I am a radiating center of Divine Light and Love, mighty to attract my good and to radiate good to others, ever-increasing joy on the planet.
— *Sunni Boehme*

My mission in life is to grow beyond the beliefs of the past and create news ones. In this I will explore all avenues to assist me in living my truth. I will help as many people as I can to do the same in which we all have a quality of life that exudes an awesome expression of God.
— *Jolly Stickley*

My mission in life is to bring love and light to others through letting the love of God change and enlighten me. I endeavor to embrace all life has to offer and leave behind more than I was given. I will live with integrity, purpose and passion and fill my life with love and laughter.
— *Dr. Ray Lueck*

I am an energized beaming light powered by *God*. I guide and inspire others through examples I set. My inner strength grows everyday and my passion for living life is infectious!
— *Shannon Carney*

Every day I want to leave everyone I cross paths with in a better state of mind.
— *Kevin Kowalke*

Write Your Life Mission Statement

Your first really "rough" draft:

_____

_____

_____

Your first revision:

_____

_____

_____

Your second revision:

_____

_____

_____

Your third revision:

_____

_____

_____

Inspired Personal Stories: Day 29

This is such a huge lesson for all of us. I would like to draw your attention to the samples of statements found on the preceding pages. I would also like you to pay special attention to David Riklan's story: he details the questions many of us have asked ourselves, and came up with quite a unique answer for himself.
— R.S.

Dear Dr. Rick,

Your lesson on mission statement made me reflect on the process I went thru a number of years ago.

I remember struggling with this as far back as the early 1980s. It was a struggle that I couldn't get away from. It kept entering my conscious mind. What am I going to do with my life? What am I supposed to do with my life? What is my purpose? What was I born to do?

I had friends who wanted to be accountants. I had friends who wanted to be doctors and lawyers. Many people I knew, or knew of, had a vision of what they wanted to do, what they wanted to be and what they wanted to accomplish.

I, on the other hand, was still struggling. What was I supposed to do? This was a struggle that was often relegated to my sub-conscious mind, but one that never went away. Life must have some purpose. It was one of the "Big Life Questions." Why are we here? But equally important was the question of, "Why am I here?"

I became more and more determined to answer this seemingly simple question, "What is my Life's Purpose?" But I felt that in order to really be able to answer this, I needed to be a better person, a smarter person, a more knowledgeable person. I would need to become a person who could answer this question.

So, my mission of self-improvement was born. If I could improve myself enough, I would be able to answer this question and find out my life's purpose. I started reading more, taking self improvement programs, Evelyn Wood, Dale Carnegie, Tony Robbins, and my quest continued.

Then, one day, I had an epiphany. My life purpose became clear. My

Life's Purpose was to figure out My Life's Purpose. I would continue to grow and to learn, and by doing so, bring myself closer to figuring out my Life's Purpose.

But for me, the challenge was how to create a life where I could continue to learn and grow. I couldn't make a living as a perpetual student. The answer finally came to me in the shape of a website called SelfGrowth.com. It would become my life and my obsession. I would build a website that provided information for people to improve their lives. It would contain articles and websites and experts, all with the unified vision of helping people improve their lives. The more resources I would find for other people to improve their lives, the more resources I would find for myself, until the day that I would figure out my true Life's Purpose.

And I realized that my Life's Purpose was born. My Life's Purpose would be to find out my Life's Purpose, and by doing so help people find theirs.

— *David Riklan, CEO, SelfGrowth.com, New Jersey*

Dear Dr. Rick,

One of the tricks I use to help me define my mission statement or what I call my "purpose" is to think like this: If I knew I had only six months to live, what would I be doing with that time? If I would want to be doing what I actually am doing, then I am "on purpose" and I have it right. If not, then back to the drawing board to redefine my purpose. For me this makes it really easy to know if I am on track or not.

— *Ella, New Buffalo, Michigan*

Dear Dr. Rick,

Your lesson about mission statement has been challenging for me! I feel like I've finally figured it out and wanted to share that with you.

Because I'm reinventing myself, your lesson was the perfect thing for me to use. But I kept feeling like I wasn't sure what I wanted to be! So, I reread your mission statement lesson a bunch of times, and I finally figured out what it meant.

Your message was "be the person you dreamed of becoming when you were a child." At first I didn't get that, because I couldn't remember dreaming of becoming anything. Not a doctor or nurse or teacher or president—nothing! I felt like it was out of my reach to figure it out.

Then, I got it! I searched in my memory for something that stood out to me from my childhood that felt really strong. That was really easy to find! I remembered that as a young girl, I read a series of books written about "The Black Stallion." Those stories brought out *so* much feeling in me! At that young age of about ten, I wanted so badly to be the main character in the book—the boy, who through love and wisdom and persistence, befriended a wild stallion and gained it's love, trust and loyalty for life. And, together they had amazing, exciting adventures, with the stallion winning races while the boy rode on his back, guiding him to his goal.

That was it! As a grown-up, I feel that feeling of love and trust through connection with other people, and help them find their way to their goals. It was so simple to find, once I really got what you were saying. Thanks!

— *Ian, Egg Harbor, Wisconsin*

Day 30

Mental Programming: Update Your Music

Today's exercise is really short, and really long. It is a very simple message that will continue to teach you to intentionally create your own environment the way *you* want it to be. Today, we address your music collection.

It is obvious that there is music that is uplifting and empowering to you ... and also music that drives you nuts, increasing your anxiety and stress level, and making you short-tempered. For most, the beloved music is from their high school and college days, whether it be the '50s, '60s, '70s, '80s, '90s, etc. It could be early rock and roll, country, jazz, new wave, pop, or folk. It could be piano, acoustic guitar, or heavy metal. There is a great variety of what can be soothing and uplifting to each unique individual.

The music that gets on your nerves is usually other people's favorite music. (Go figure.) It could be the favorite tunes of your kids, your parents, your roommate who grew up in New Orleans, your spouse who happens to be from Nashville, the country music capital of the world ... you get the idea. How many times have our parents asked us to "turn that racket off"?

The first part of the exercise is obvious: have music around you that is uplifting. This means music with both positive sounds and positive lyrical messages. Okay, try this: play as many songs with messages of love as you can! Think also about love of humanity. Consider "Amazing Grace," "What a Wonderful World," "Everything Is Beautiful" ... the list of love songs continues infinitely.

Secondly, if you would like a more empirical guide to selecting positive music, Dr. David Hawkins has used kinesiology to rate music, both artists and genres, on a scale. On his scale of one to one thousand, two hundred is the neutral point, with anything above being positive emotionally and anything below being negative. On his scale, six hundred and above represents enlightenment, with one thousand representing God-consciousness.

You can find this "musical scale," which he calls the "energy of music," on page 97 of Dr. Hawkins' book *Truth vs. Falsehood*.

The following is an excerpt of some of his ratings. Interpret them using the scale as defined above and see if you agree with Dr. Hawkins' assessment:

The Energy of Music

Gangster Rap: 35
Heavy Metal: 95
Pop Rock: 205
Disco: 235
Country Western: 255

Rolling Stones: 340
Elvis: 420
The Beatles: 460
Ray Charles: 485
Santana: 515
Bach: 530
George Harrison: 540
Mozart: 540
Christmas Carols: 550
The song "Amazing Grace": 575
Pachelbel's "Canon in D": 690!

Consider shifting as much of your musical exposure as you can. Perhaps skip the Rap concert and play some sweet songs on the piano, guitar, or CD player, or even go to a symphony. I believe you still get the exposure to the positive energy, even if you doze off!

Who knew that your next assignment would be to go listen to Pachelbel's Canon?

Remember to let it into your heart, then you will start to make it better.
— The Beatles, "Hey Jude"

Inspired Personal Stories: Day 30

Hi Rick,

There has always been music playing in the background of the happiest and some of the earliest memories of my life. Every time you hear that one song, lyric or riff, you're right back there feeling that original feeling of joy. For instance, whenever I hear "Philadelphia Freedom" by Elton John, it takes me back to when I was a little girl and I would hop in the back seat of my mom's 1971 Chevy Impala to go to my aunt and uncle's house for a Saturday barbeque. Or "Redemption Song" by Bob Marley: "It's only ourselves that can free our minds." This song was playing in the background as our son was being born and whenever I hear it, I'm filled mind, body and soul with deep love and gratitude.

Whenever I exercise or compete athletically, I play the type of music that both fires me up and helps me to focus. When I'm looking to achieve a task, I call upon the classical genre and somehow the procrastination goes away.

When I look at my playlist, I wonder if somehow I just created the sound track to my life!

— *Annie Ovans, Bay View, Wisconsin*

Hi Rick,

When I read your Day 30 lesson, it reverberated fully through me. Positive music! After all, my blood type is B Positive ... (get it? "be positive?") ... really!

Simplicity is part of what makes for a less stressful life, which helps with staying upbeat and positive but music ... oh music! It has the ability to lift one's spirits higher than just caffeine or an endorphin rush after a run.

As of this writing, I have 704 songs captured in iTunes. Nearly three-quarters of them have positive, life affirming lyrics. Any instrumentals have to be either fast moving, or the few that tap the foot a bit slower need an emotional touch to them. Tears can be uplifting, too, if they're from good memories ... and the soundtracks, the powerful soundtracks. Have you ever walked out of a movie theater so on top of the world because you were taken to another time and place, feeling as though anything was possible? Did you realize that music played a big part of that movie?

This world is so full of wonderful choices, all we need to do is *choose!* Choose to play your own positive, uplifting, life affirming music and it can change your perspective even during the darkest of times.

Music to the ear, set between "Fly Me to the Moon," "Fly like an Eagle," "America the Beautiful" and "Seasons of Love" from the musical *Rent.* From "Sweet Home Alabama" to "Sweet Home Chicago," "Georgia on My Mind" to "California Dreamin,' " "Higher Ground," "Believe," "Celebrate Me Home," "Better Together," "Can't Keep It In," "I Feel Free," "Eyes on the Prize," "Beauty in the World," "Better Version of Me," "Into the Light," "Out of the Blue," "Let's Dance" ... I think you get the idea.

So go ahead, choose to listen to things that lift you to a higher ground and start seeing the world around you in a different light.

— *Chris Wacker, Investment Advisor, Milwaukee, Wisconsin*

Doc,

When I read your lesson for Day 30, I think you totally missed the boat on this one. I was totally in touch with the idea of the power of mental programming with the music you hear. What immediately came to mind reading the lesson was the lack of any mention of creating music. I believe this is equally important.

I have worked in marketing, in advertising, and have helped deliver messages by adding copyrighted music and creating my own musical soundtracks. I also have worked extensively with at-risk kids, and there I have always used the power of creating music as a positive teaching tool. I really believe this should not be overlooked in this lesson.

I agree that when listening, pick music that will lift you up, why not? But don't stop there. Get involved in the creative process. Anyone can sit down at a piano and pick out something that sounds good to their ear, no matter how simple. Create it. Enjoy it. The rush and the "lifting up" will intensify when one is involved in the creative process. Trust me.

— *Patrick Sheedy, professional musician, marketing consultant, Hartland, Wisconsin*

Day 31

Diet, Nutrition and Weight Loss:
Practice Losing the Fear

Diet and Nutrition are continually some of the hottest topics on our minds and emphasized in our culture. Putting diet and your physical body back in balance can seem overwhelming, but is really a very simple thing. Let me give you some background so we can transform our thinking together before we get to the Action Step for today.

There is an absolutely genius design behind all living things. Look at a tulip, a willow tree, a mosquito, a hummingbird, a gazelle, and a whale. All of these living organisms are in perfect balance. They live totally in the present moment, and completely follow their cravings. Each is given the exact intelligence to guide them to their perfect diet. There are plants and trees that live perfectly in each climate. There are insects and animals that live perfectly in each climate. They are all designed and built to thrive in their respective environments. And the planet provides them with everything that they need in order to be in balance.

Humans are in the exact same position. We are designed and built to physically thrive. And similarly, the planet provides us with everything we need. The only difference between us and the rest of creation is that we have the ability to screw up this natural balance with our thinking. We are able to reflect on the past, worry about the future, and totally question and have anxiety in the present. All this over-thinking takes us out of our natural state of thriving. A major culprit in this imbalance is the message of fear that is constantly bombarding us from every direction. These messages come from the newspaper, the TV, commercials, our families and friends, the medical community, and the countless companies that are shamelessly promoting their product, using whatever information they can find to reach their bottom line.

Messages of fear and anxiety regarding diet and health have evolved to the point of creating visible fear in the faces of shoppers in the grocery store. These worried consumers are frantically reading nutrition fact labels while trying to remember all of the things they have been taught to avoid. They are also reading the marketing slogans on the products and constantly buying in to the fact that our bodies need something to fulfill whatever it is the product claims they lack. That fear motivates us to consume certain products because we believe our bodies are dangerously lacking what they offer. Some current examples of this thinking include the messages about anti-oxidants to battle all that is toxic all around us (including the sun), or germicidal sprays to battle all the invisible, evil bacteria and viruses closing in on us.

Let's think about this for a minute—our bodies are filled with millions of microorganisms, all with the perfect intelligence to create a perfect symbiotic balance. All we need to do is just *trust* it. Trust it! Our bodies know how to deliver oxygen to every cell, how to control breathing and circulation, how to transmit billions of electrical and chemical messages per minute. How could any scientist or doctor think they know what's right for our bodies better than the innate intelligence of our bodies themselves?

How much did we know about microbiology and nutritional biochemistry two hundred years ago? How about two thousand years ago? Think about how much we have learned and discovered in the past twenty years alone, and how much less we knew then, and how ill-equipped we supposedly were to choose our own proper nutrition. It sounds ridiculous, but the vitamin companies and food industry would have you believe it. The worrisome catch is that with that thinking, twenty years from now we will be looking back and be convinced about how unprepared we were to choose proper nutrition today.

I suggest that you quiet all that noise. New conclusions and cultural messages are forever going to change decade by decade, and therefore have no true long-lasting value. Instead of buying into temporary beliefs and ideas, let's condense all of this commotion down to *simple, timeless truth*. The ultimate truth is that our bodies, just like those of the plants and animals, already have *all* the programming and intelligence inside of them that is needed to thrive. Trust them. Follow your cravings. Trust your body!

Here is the core truth about diet and nutrition: *It is not what you eat—it is how you feel about what you eat!*

Did you know that in an experiment rabbits that were force-fed super high cholesterol diets developed high rates of heart attacks? Except for a group of animals that was cuddled and petted prior to being fed. These rabbits, in a more peaceful emotional state, were able to actually physically metabolize the cholesterol differently!

Your beliefs about food and nutrition inevitably match up with your body's behaviors. You certainly know someone who says, "I can eat anything I want and never gain a pound." You also know someone who says, "no matter how little I eat, I can't lose weight." Did you ever notice that as these beliefs are affirmed, that person's body continues to fulfill that pattern?

Trust your body's inherent wisdom and listen to your cravings. If you are craving red meat, eat it. If you are craving fruit, or beets, or carrots, eat them. If you are craving a jelly donut, eat it. Trust that your body, in its infinite intelligence, will know what to do with it.

Let's go back to the plant and animal kingdoms again. There are no messages of fear of science or marketing, just simply pure instincts and cravings. My best recommendation to you is to quiet all the outside noise and pay attention to your inner instincts and cravings. Each of us as a human being is equipped with everything we need inside us to thrive.

Here is the Action Step for today: quiet all the external messages coming to you about diet and nutrition. Listen solely to your inner cravings today. Do not consume anything at all based on fear messages, or what you have been told you are "supposed" to eat. Listen solely to your inner cravings. When you choose a food, recite this affirmation: "My physical body, in its infinite intelligence, will know exactly what to do with this in order to provide me with the greatest benefit." Recite that affirmation around each thing you consume today. Carry that idea with you at all times.

The way you look at diet and nutrition will be completely transformed as you learn to give your body the authority and freedom that it needs in order to sustain itself, rather than giving your power away to external voices and messages. You will find over time that your diet will change according to your inner cravings, you will continue to grow healthier, have more energy, have more clarity of thought, sleep better, and be more physically fit. How's that for a nice little side-effect?!

It's not WHAT you eat, it's how you FEEL about what you eat.

Inspired Personal Stories: Day 31

Dr. Rick,

My daughter, Allison, was diagnosed with Type 1 diabetes when she was eight years old. This meant she had to give herself daily insulin shots for the rest of her life, while carefully regulating her food intake and exercise.

The beautiful thing is that she never complained and was a picture of health throughout her time at home. Interestingly, when my wife and I met people who knew Allison, their most common comment was "Allison is always so happy." We think that had a lot to do with her great health.

Anyway, following high school, she left Milwaukee to go to Georgetown University in Washington DC—and, frankly, we were a bit worried.

She was going to be all by herself in brand new surrounding and we were sure that everyone would have advice for what she should eat or not eat, given her diabetes.

We had seen this her whole life up until that point. The media, friends, teachers, and even strangers all felt the need to question what she was eating ("Can you have that?"), tell her what she shouldn't eat ("We aren't serving desert because of your illness"), or give advice for what she should eat (usually based on some news report they just saw on TV).

While she was home, we could counter all of that nonsense with our own advice—"ignore what everyone else is telling you and just pay attention to what your own body is telling you."

We had met a diabetic educator in Allison's early years who told us that diabetes was a lifelong experiment—but with just one subject. And, we took this to heart. We knew that only Allison could figure out what was going on in her own body and, as long as she paid attention to it and trusted what she was feeling, she would do great.

Well, that's exactly what happened. She headed off to college confident that she could ignore all of the external advice and just trust the brilliance of her own body.

Allison is now 24, works as a healthcare consultant, runs half-marathons—and we're still told by people who meet her that "she always seems so happy."

This is Day 31 in successful action. It's right to say, "The ultimate truth is that our bodies, just like those of the plants and animals, already have all the programming and intelligence inside of them that is needed to thrive. Trust them. Follow your cravings. Trust your body!"

The human body is an extraordinarily complicated and brilliant piece of work. So complicated that it's impossible for *anyone* else to know what is good or bad for it and so brilliant that, if you just trust it, you'll be fine.
— *Allen O., Seattle, Washington*

Hi Rick!

I completely agree with you. Babies are born with the ability to eat only what they need, they do not over-eat. That is a learned behavior taught to them by parents insisting they eat everything on their plate (even though they didn't select what or how much is on their plate). As a parent, I refuse to force my children to eat, I let them gauge their own intake. What I learned from this day, though, is that as much as I am trying to help my children be okay with what they eat and how much, I am not allowing myself that same luxury. I will try to treat myself in this way as well as I treat my children.
— *Alicia, West Bend, Wisconsin*

Day 32

Alleviating Worry and Living in the Now: Take a Walk

Eckhart Tolle, among many others, has written volumes on staying in the Now. He teaches us that worry is nothing more than negative, wasted energy about future possibilities that may never happen. Similarly bound to our thoughts, the past is simply our re-creation of an event according to our memories. Because they are both bound up in our minds, we have no external control over the future or the past. Ultimately, both are born in the imagination, and bound by the creativity with which we see them. If we focus on either, we miss the present moment—which is the only place we can truly experience joy and fulfillment. The present is all that you have. Don't miss it!

Looking back, don't you wish you would have had the wisdom to enjoy and appreciate your childhood a lot more? How about your twenties or your thirties? In this same way, someday you will be looking back on this time in your life, and wishing you would have appreciated it more. So don't let a moment of "NOW" pass you by!

For me, the simplest way to connect to that "now" energy is to take a walk. Feel the immediacy of nature, the weather, the earth, the sun, and the sky. Feel the magnitude of your surroundings and how it calmly confirms the existence of a higher power, an infinite intelligence.

Picture the planet revolving in perfectly planned orbit around the sun, while rotating exactly on its axis. Ponder the massive oak trees and the delicate flowers that exist solely for the purpose of bringing beauty into our lives. Tune in to the movement of the ladybugs, the ants, the birds, and the squirrels. Perfection is all around you!

Now, if you can, go barefoot in the grass and face the sun. Close your eyes, and feel the warm sun saturating the skin of your face. Feel the clean breeze refresh your skin, and the cool grass between your toes. Embrace the recognition of this pure and simple perfection, connecting you completely with the NOW!

Action Step: Use going for a walk, however brief, to remind you of the immediate presence of the world around you and connect you with the present moment. Go for a five minute walk today, and every day thereafter!

Every path leads back to more YOU.
— R.S.

Inspired Personal Stories: Day 32

Hi Rick!

I really like the Take a Walk day. I have been walking my kids to school and back now and I love it! My older daughter and I stop to smell the lilacs, we talk about the different houses, dogs, plants, etc. that we see on the way, and even though it's the same walk every day we still find new things to talk about and look at! Even my six month old loves the walks!

— *Joy L., West Bend, Wisconsin*

Dear Rick,

The walk for Day 32 is a great boost for the senses and the mind. Each day and season brings out different experiences. I never follow the same path twice in a row, or go out at the same time when I walk, this way I know I can experience a new perspective of the surroundings and my current now.

A morning walk might lead me through large puddles on the sidewalk from sprinklers, afternoon or evening might have the neighbors out walking their dogs or working in their yards. In winter, a fresh snowfall brings more beauty to the walk

— *Jason Stein, Sturgeon Bay, WI*

Hi Dr. Rick,

Living in the now is a very difficult attitude to establish. And, it is just that, an attitude. It's a habit driven by one's personal priorities, which are formed by experiences.

One most excellent experience I had came in September of 1997. This day, I succeeded in "living in the now" and even "savored the moment." I had been associated with a relationship marketing company, where independent business owners earned income by offering products through their teams of other enrolled representatives. To be super successful (which I was blessed to be), one had to travel a lot. Emails, Skype, cell phones where merely dreams at the time. I was so driven to get rich, that I often left my wife, Lucie, with the daily responsibility of raising our four kids. This was not an easy task, since she was without an instruction booklet to help her. That was our price to pay, as I tried to achieve financial freedom. One very huge reward came at a national conference in September, 1997, when Lucie received the very first of an award given, (voted by our fellow representatives) called the "Most Supportive Partner" award.

She was surprised and shocked, as she stepped to the stage to be recognized and greeted by 13,000 encouraging, screaming and applauding representatives and friends. With my arms filled with red roses, I greeted her with a whisper to "savor the moment," all to the music of artist Vince Gill's hit, "I Still Believe in You," filling our hearts and souls with excitement, and sharing with all who were present that moment at the Dallas Reunion Arena.

Savor the moment ... those are magical words to live by. While standing on the arena stage, she and I were definitely "living in the now." We are able to recount that special moment thanks to technology and video, but it lives most vividly in our memories.

My life has contained many God blessed moments, but through that one unexpected occurrence, I became better at "living in the now."

For the record, I learned and practiced the value of "savoring the moment" from wearing out tapes and CDs by Zig Ziglar, while traveling those thousands of miles of the early years of my life's journey. I continue to work on living in the now, so if and when we meet, slow down please, so I may savor that moment as well. Let's make our time count.

— *Phil Mims, President, Nussentials Corp., Houston, Texas*

Dr. Rick,

Your take a walk day is so easy! I recently took a walk with a friend, and we focused on what it feels like to be fully present in the now moment. As we walked, we talked about what it feels like to be in our bodies, and to be aware of our surroundings. It was really awesome, because our awareness of everything around us grew and grew and it made us start laughing just by feeling happy!

We progressed from taking in the beauty of the summer flowers, the beautiful sky and the feel of the evening air, to acknowledging the amazement of simply touching the hand of another. Wow, were we on a high! It was so great! And it made us want to keep doing that with anything and everything we could see or think of!

It led us back to ourselves! What fun!

— *Eileen, Port Washington, Wisconsin*

Day 33

Restoring Your Health:
The Infinite Intelligence of Your Body
and the True Cause of Disease

I want you to realize that disease and health are easily manageable issues. They, like everything else, can be shifted massively by slight adjustments in your thoughts.

Curing your cancer is no more difficult to achieve than getting along with your teenage daughter when she stays out past curfew, which is no more difficult than leaving a $5 tip for a $3 cup of coffee, not checking email until noon, or sending a card of appreciation each day. *Every* thing in this physical world is a small thing. Changing any of these things just requires a shift in thinking. Sometimes a change in your thinking may feel like a dramatic overnight quantum leap, but each lasting shift is actually a series of baby shifts, most of which occur unobserved below the surface.

By focusing on the Action Steps and Lessons in Days 1 through 32 of this program, you have already laid a lot of the groundwork to be ready to make a quantum leap in the way you look at disease and your health.

There are so many opinions out there on the treatment of disease: drugs, surgery, nutrition, vitamins, cleansing, chiropractic, acupuncture, essential oils, and eastern philosophies. It can be overwhelming to consider. Which of these approaches is the *real* truth? Is there one best right answer for each disease? The answer to this question is YES—it is the one that you *believe* will work best for you!

There is no one right physical answer because every interaction with disease is different. Two people exposed to HIV, two people stepping on a rusty nail, two people smoking for forty years can all have completely different results. There is no blamable pathogen that causes disease—there are just susceptible hosts. It is not what you are exposed to; it is your set of thoughts and beliefs that determines your health!

There are people that have cured themselves of cancer by eating macrobiotic diets, by exercising, by laughing their way through Marx Brothers movies, or by sending joy to others. There are also those that have cured themselves with chemotherapy and surgery. Dr. Deepak Chopra and Dr. Bernie Siegel speak of many examples of healing just through the shifting of a patient's thoughts and beliefs. The foundation of their success begins with the basic principle that our body's natural state is that of wellness.

Here is the key: your behavior must match your belief. If you think you need a drug or surgery to cure your disease, and you truly believe it will work, then you best travel that route. If you truly believe that you don't need those things, then take that route. No pathogen infects one hundred percent of its hosts, and no pharmaceutical drug or surgery works in one hundred percent of patients either. It always has to be a match. Over time, transforming your beliefs by practicing new thoughts will be your most reliable route. If you create a new habit of thought, you will create a new belief; and then you can invite in new behaviors about health and disease, with those new behaviors eventually matching up with your new beliefs.

Ultimately you must take personal responsibility for your own health from the inside, acknowledging that your wellness is a result of your own creation. If you choose to hand over that personal responsibility to an outside person to "fix" your body's ailment, it will simply recur or transfer to another area of your body. I have witnessed this innumerable times in my twenty years of medical practice.

I have two great gifts for you today for your Action Step. The first is to practice a simple shift of thinking around your health. If your left wrist has pain, shift your focus onto your right wrist and appreciate how wonderful it feels. If you right knee is sore while walking or running, shift your attention onto your left knee and appreciate how perfectly it functions. If you have a headache, shift your attention onto your feet and how strongly they support and transport your body from place to place. You may be really surprised to see how well this works, because of the universal truth that pain cannot persist in the absence of a suffering response. So instead of creating a welcoming environment for the pain, respond with appreciation and love for your body. Try it, and be amazed!

The second gift is that of two long lost cures: air and water! Remember, it is not the drug or the surgery that cures, but it is how your belief matches up with the treatment. Amazing deep breathing and satisfying drinks of good clear water can be miracles for you if you choose for them to be. When you need an upward shift in your physical or mental well-being, take five deep breaths, slowly and deliberately, and put all of your attention on the healing you expect to find in those deep breaths. It really works!

Take a bottle of water and label it. Write on it "headache medicine," or "strong healthy back" water, or "run faster" water, or "better tennis serve" water. How does that sound? Forget the pill, and just label a bottle of water! You can even label the water with a simple word representing an emotion like love, peacefulness, joy appreciation, or happiness. Drink the water and focus on the healing emotion.

This technique will continue to work better and better as you hone your focus. When you have a headache, simply grab a bottle of water and trust that it will take care of it. If your back is sore, do the same. It will work. Practice it! You can even teach it to your kids. If they've been taught to believe that going to the doctor will make them feel better, they can certainly believe that water and air will work just as well, if you stick with the thought shift together.

For additional information on the fascinating topic of health and disease, read the works of the experts cited above or do some online searches of your own. I also recommend Dr. Masaru Emoto's *The True Power of Water*, and the Louise Hay's *You Can Heal Your Body*. Overriding your past beliefs about what brings you health and what rids you of disease will take patience and practice, but continuing to consume information about this topic will help you in the process of retraining your thoughts.

Nerves that fire together, wire together.
— Dr. Joe Dispenza

Finally, remember it is not about the "right" treatment, it is not about the cure, and it is not even about prevention. Good health is about doing the work on the inside, at the root level of the *cause* of illness: your thoughts. Transform them into positive confident thoughts of wellness, and live a Maximum Life!

I spent four years medical school learning the symptoms of disease. Now I know disease itself to be the real symptom, and if you don't address the real cause, don't worry ... it'll get worse.
— R.S.

Inspired Personal Stories: Day 33

I'd like to introduce this section by reminding you that there is no one single best answer to your health issues or questions. It all depends what thought you are within reach of and what action matches perfectly with your belief right now. Over time you can always work towards evolving it along whatever path you desire.

I hope in the future we can fill a whole book to share with Inspired Personal Stories of Health.

— R.S.

Hi Rick,

I want to share my experience with Day 33.

One of my physical issues is joint pain in the knees. I've worked on that for a while, but have gotten discouraged as it seems to get progressively worse.

While doing the self-love writing, I found myself scribbling down, without hesitation: "I love my knees." I almost laughed out loud at how ridiculous that sounded when I'd actually been getting angry that these knees were causing me such pain and restriction. Since then, and quite quickly, my knee pain has diminished remarkably!

As a naturopathic doctor, it is a blessing that I will share with many others. What fun! Thanks.

— Dr. Gael Riverz, ND/Iridologist, Delafield, WI

Dr. Rick,

Your profound statement, "your behavior must match your belief," solidifies even more my decision to use alternative treatment for my breast cancer that was diagnosed three years ago. I had the surgeries and elected to do breast reconstruction and while I was in recovery mode, I read up on alternatives vs. standard care. After visits with two oncologists and radiologists, I felt that chemo and radiation wasn't in sync with my core.

I worked with a naturopathic doctor and am doing a lot to rebuild my immune system, including going on a vegetarian diet. My learning journey on alternatives continues to this day. I share a lot with my

friends and family members about what I learn to help instill the value of what we choose to eat and think. There is so much to be said about how we think and the potential toll it can take on our bodies. Thankfully, there's an abundance of info on the Internet regarding a multitude of self-healing modalities. I have gained so much from it all.
— *Diane, Columbus, Ohio*

Hi Dr. Rick,

I have been experiencing fibromyalgia and osteoarthritis for approximately ten years. I know these are inflammation problems and that my anxiousness and tension are causing them. I take only natural supplements for them. I think I am on the right track to get better by focusing on so many positive messages, and I feel my thoughts changing over time to be more optimistic. *Thank* you for reinforcing what I already "know". I *know* I can finally take charge of my health in a *much bigger* way by removing *my* stuck thoughts/beliefs.
— *Barb, Charlotte, North Carolina*

Dear Rick,

I was very sick for over five years during which a change in medication nearly cost me my life, and left me brain damaged.

I became a vegetable. Specialists told me I would never work again and I would be on medication for life. It's really a good thing I didn't believe them! Instead, I worked on the things that I needed to do to recover, and I really worked on taking charge of my health and took full responsibility for everything that happened, including the idea that my thoughts affected my recovery. I even learned to read and write again—an interesting experience when you are a qualified Early Childhood teacher.

I am now medication-free and have worked in Tertiary Education for almost a year teaching Life Skills, Math and Language to Asian adults. I believe my health continues to benefit from my positive thoughts. Cheers.
— *Gemma Ward, New Zealand*

Hi Dr. Rick,

I want to share a personal story of a friend of mine, who refused to let doctors tell him their statistics.

Sandy was a man who lived a simple childhood. Growing up on a farm meant that summers were spent helping with the corn crops, especially with the "de-tasselling" part. He worked under the summer sun, shirtless, soaking in the warmth.

When his daughter was six months old, he had surgery to remove the melanoma growth on his back. The doctors told him that he was lucky to have the "best" situation of something that is very, very bad. They expected to see him back within a few years.

But ten years went by without incident. Sandy focused on his belief in the wellness genius of his body. Then, one day he noticed a lump under his arm. Series of medical visits followed; surgery. He and his wife were told he'd best get his life together because he had six months to live.

But he wouldn't listen, and he spent the next five years not listening to their dire predictions—and he never allowed them to say what his statistical chances of survival were.

Throughout the journey, he played tennis (he was very competitive), he rode his bike, he exercised, he continued running his company. He wouldn't speak of the illness, he always spoke of his health and the ability of his body to regenerate itself. The doctors caring for him were confounded and couldn't explain the phenomenon that he was. When they told him cancer was "eating" his wrist, he went out and played more tennis. They put a cast on his wrist when it became fractured, and one week later it was completely healed. There was no medical explanation for his continued health—or his even being alive.

Although he passed five years later, the "mystery" was that he even lived that long, and that he lived fully. Many people were completely unaware that he was ill, because he didn't talk about it. Sandy had unshakable belief in the genius of his wellness, he filled his body with the fresh air and exercise he loved, and he had the intuition to not put his focus, or anyone else's focus, on the illness. What a wise teacher he was.
— *Mary Jane, Dixon, Illinois*

Hi Rick,

I love the lesson on health. For some people, kicking all of their medications may not be a big deal, but for me that was huge! I had felt that ever since I had gotten on my medications ten years ago, I was putting poison in my body because the medications didn't cure me, they would just mask whatever I was having an issue with. I was having stomach problems and ulcers, and really bad allergies. My medications would work and then all of a sudden they would stop working, which triggered me to take more.

At first I just saw it as a necessity, and there was no other way around it. I realized after seven years it was getting to the point where the relief that I felt was getting shorter and shorter, which meant that I either had to take more or put up with it, and neither of those were fascinating options. Then I finally decided that I was going to take the all natural route and I started to eat all organic and natural foods, and take vitamins and supplements. I did a body cleanse, which allowed me to get all of the toxins out of my liver and my entire body.

And I tell you, having the guts to do that and have a major life shift changed my life, because I haven't taken medications since 2007. I'm 37 now, I feel like I'm ten years younger and I feel healthy; my mind is more alert, I'm happier, and eat whatever I want now. I really believe that had I not made that mental shift, and the dedication to do it, I would be a mess today.

Before, I felt like as the years went on, I was literally losing my life. Now I feel I have my life back.

I don't want to go to the doctor anymore because I just don't feel they're going to do anything for me. They're not going to fix anything, they're just going to prescribe some medication all over again. I've been there ... that's not going to fix anything!
— *Kevin Kowalke, Lead Strategist, The Kowalke Group, Brookfield, Wisconsin*

The doctor of the future will give no medication, but will interest his patients in the care of the human frame, in diet, and in the cause and prevention of disease.
— *Thomas Alva Edison*

Day 34

Endless Possibilities:
Hang a Blank Canvas

Throughout this program, we have recognized together the significance of surrounding ourselves with positive images. We have also begun to focus on creating our worlds the way we desire them to be. In today's powerful exercise, we will combine both!

As you spend more and more time with these concepts, allowing them to sink deeper into your being, you will require fewer and fewer external triggers to create joy, and you will be able to simply conjure up joy from inside yourself. Today's Action Step assists you in doing that.

Choose a prominent wall in your home—the living room walls or the wall above your bed are great choices. Remove anything currently hanging there. Now, imagine if you had the perfect beautiful, new, original painting; what size would you desire it to be? Great—now we need to go on an errand!

Head out to the local artist supply store and pick out a blank artist's canvas of that size. Return home and hang it in the place you determined. Now step back and admire the pure potentiality of this canvas.

What is the first image you see there? Keep looking. Feel the brilliance of the colors, the sweeping finesse of the brush strokes, and the emotion of the composition. Imagine increasingly profound and personal art. Can you see an artist's rendering of your kids joyfully playing with each other? Can you see a friend cheerfully helping you with something really meaningful to you? Can you see yourself accepting the gleaming gold trophy for winning a golf tournament? Can you see the masterpiece of Van Gogh's "Starry Night"? The "Mona Lisa"? Andy Warhol's "Campbell's Soup Can"? Your favorite sunrise memory? Your favorite mountain range? Can you see your child proudly showing off their newest clay sculpture from art class in elementary school? Can you see your spouse embracing you and gazing at you with eyes so deep with love that they open right into their soul? Can you see it?

As you admire and imagine, anything you choose to put your attention on can appear on the canvas. There are infinite, unlimited possibilities. Over time, you may come to like this picture better than any other in your home. The creative always gives more life than the already created. Potentiality is more invigorating than the already discovered and accomplished.

Another advantage of this canvas may be that it becomes one of your favorite "conversation starters" in your entire home. You will have a great learning experience showing it to guests and asking them what they envision. You may be surprised to observe the ways some people's thoughts are limited to what they have already seen, and how others find it natural to be innovative. It may reveal a lot about the minds of your friends and family!

Have fun with it, and see just how creative you can be. This canvas is like your ever-changing, ever-perfect genie board. Limitlessness always provides magic!

Most people spend their whole lives looking in the wrong direction. They are looking out instead of looking in.
— R.S.

Inspired Personal Stories: Day 34

Dear Rick,

The day I bought a blank canvas, I had a very unexpected emotional experience. It was a surprise because I had known about the concept for quite a while and had many experiences of exposure to a blank canvas in another person's home which seemed to represent what it felt like to gaze at one.

As it turns out, it wasn't the same at all! I went to the local artists' supply store to choose one, and as I was looking at the different sizes available, a feeling starting coming up inside me that was a sense of anticipation. That alone was unexpected! I realized that there's some part of me that's longing to experience more *life,* and it was getting excited that this blank canvas is the starting point. It was really cool!

So, as I was looking at the sizes, an image came into my mind. It was a countryside scene in France, with rolling hills, purple flowers— heather, I think—green and yellow accents weaving through the purple, and blue sky with white clouds. I have no idea why that image came up because I've never been to France and it isn't one of my life goals to go there. But, it came up. So I began looking at these canvases with the question in my mind "is this one big enough to hold the dream, the vision, of my life?" It was such a great question to ask, because I became acutely aware that I have such a strong, deep desire for every component of my life to grow and be so much bigger and better than it is now. And the blank canvas allows me to change the image on the canvas anytime I want. It allows me to let all of my current visions be a piece of artwork, and to keep dreaming new dreams and imagining them into live form.

I settled on a size that felt right to me, brought it home and hung in it a room where I can see it often. So far, each time I look at it, I get this really cool feeling in my body that makes me smile. I'm making it a point to meditate on it every day for at least a few minutes, creating images about things that I desire to experience.

I think that the most significant thing about that experience was that such a strong feeling rose up inside me when I actually made the purchase of a blank canvas for *myself.* It didn't work for me to have it

be someone else's; it had to be my own. That seems a bit weird to me, because why not have my imagination in place on any blank canvas, but apparently I needed my own. I bet now that I've opened to that feeling inside me, it's going to work anywhere and everywhere.
— *Judy Corkle, Life Coach, Chicago, Illinois*

Nothing is the new something.
— *R.S.*

Day 35

Embracing Diversity:
Live in a World of
Seven Billion Perspectives

What is the difference between the real world (the physical world around you) and a dream world (the world that you envision)? My belief is that there is no difference. Consider this: there are roughly seven billion people on this planet. Each of us sees the world through our own eyes, limited to our own physical bodies. We live in a certain area of the planet, with our own culture, family, climate, geography, traditions, and habits. We certainly all have our own unique personalities. So in effect, we all have a slightly different reality.

Without a doubt, no two of us think in exactly the same way. We range from having slightly varying thoughts about some things to having completely opposite opinions about others. The beliefs we have come from the habit of thought that we keep practicing.

The world is the same for everyone looking at it: the universe is the same for everyone; and God, the universal power, the infinite intelligence, is also the same for all. Yet we are all looking at these realities from differing perspectives.

Therefore, the reality that each of us experiences is nothing more than a variation—it is an experience colored by the bias of our own thoughts, perspectives, beliefs, and personality. This perspective, this interpretation, and these thoughts are all a personal creation of our own selves. In effect, we are creating every aspect of our reality.

So my question to you is this: If you are creating your reality, why not create it according to the way you truly desire it to be? If you are going to live in a world of your own creation, why not create it in alignment with your dreams? I refer to this concept as your "dream world," and I suggest that you live in it!

Go back and read what you wrote for the exercise in Day 23: The Perfect Day. Recall that you can create every last bit of that day and the feelings associated with it if you choose to keep it in your thoughts. It will be real for you! You have probably heard the saying, "it's not what happens to you, it is your attitude about what happens to you." This principle affirms the power that you have to create your own reality.

Try these Action Steps, just to be playful, and see what happens. Add $50,000 to your checkbook register. Imagine everything not the way you've come to expect it to be, but the way you desire it to be. Write your name with the degree you want. Add stuff to your genie board. Laugh with someone you struggle with. Try anything. Hey, it's your dream. Imagine your dream world, and then live in it!

Some people live in reality. Some people live in a dream world. My goal is to help you turn one into the other.
— R.S.

Inspired Personal Stories: Day 35

Dear Dr. Rick,

Day 35 brought a wonderful awareness to me that I want to share with you. The lesson itself is so great, in encouraging us to use our unique perspective on our life experiences to become conscious creators. I love that! It is so empowering, and each day I use that exercise many times.

I now have an awareness that every single person has the same paradigm—that they can only see life through their own eyes, and no one else's. Wow, that is a big concept to think about! In our world where we are taught to expect everyone to see things the same way, this is a big change and gosh is it helpful! Suddenly, we can have more acceptance of ourselves, and others, if we realize and remember that the *only* way we can see life is through our own eyes and no one else's!

Besides being a lesson in consciousness creating, I believe this to also have an added dimension of self-love. What could be more loving of ourself than to be at ease with others' views exactly as they are? Seven billion perspectives means no one is right, and no one is wrong. How great to hold that feeling!

— *Marissa Winston, Cedar Rapids, Iowa*

There are four worlds: the mental, the emotional, the spiritual, and the physical. The physical world is simply a "printout" of the other three.

—*T. Harv Ecker, author,* **Secrets of the Millionaire Mind**

Day 36

Wealth Consciousness II: Allowing in Unlimited Income

"Finally!" you say. Yes, we are finally ready to address the topic of money together! Looking back, you can see that we have actually been working with money throughout this program. You have completed exercises in giving gifts, tips, charity, trusting the universe to provide for you, even giving away your last $5. All of these exercises have helped you diminish your anxieties and expand your thoughts about money.

There has probably been more thought-programming in your life about money than any other topic, so don't be discouraged if your thoughts about it don't seem to shift as quickly or easily as you would like. You have been trained to think that money is a finite resource your entire life. However, I believe that if you look deep inside, you intuition already knows that money is an infinite resource.

You have seen endless examples of this. Look at the $72 million Nike contract offered to LeBron James right out of high school. Look at the music scene, where a newcomer in Hip Hop can literally make millions. Look at bankruptcy, which can increase one's net worth by hundreds of thousands of dollars ... instantly! Look at the young people with brand new business ideas that after just a few years get bought up for millions of dollars. These examples suggest that incredible abundance is possible, and can appear as a response to any impetus, no matter how improbable.

Money is like water: it needs to keep flowing to hold its beneficial energy. If it is left stagnant, it will become stale and be of no benefit to anyone. If you choose to see money as a limited resource, you will experience greed and jealousy and will have an instinct to hoard whatever money comes to you. The energy of money becomes stagnant and stale and only brews negativity when it is subject to the hoarding impulse. Ten dollars passed to one person that is stopped and hoarded has far less energy than ten dollars passed from person to person, over and over, in exchange for goods and services or in simple acts of kindness and generosity. Keeping money flowing keeps its energy high and keeps your abundance flowing. As a person who keeps the energy of money moving, you will be able to allow more and more of it in. *The more you give away, the more you will be provided with.*

If you see money as an infinite resource, you will be able to keep it moving; adding energy to it as it passes through your hands, doing great things in the world with it, and giving life to others who can spend the same dollars again and again. You will continually create a space in which more money can find you, and you will in turn be able to spend it and give it away in any amount for anything you choose. The Law of Attraction states that what you give away will be returned to you many fold. Following this principle, it you want more money to come in, send more money out. You will find that more and more will continually find you if you can keep the energy alive and moving.

Like everything else we've learned, *it's not how much money you have, it's how you feel about the money you do have.*

So let's give this thinking a shot. I have an Action Step for you that is a baby step that can lay the groundwork for future huge changes in the way you feel about money, and in turn open up great channels for abundance to flow to you. We will replace some tiny fears and programmed responses about money with some open, trusting, flowing thoughts.

Today's exercise requires that you take out a pad of paper to retrain you thoughts like you did for Day 28 Exercise and Fitness. Write across the top, "I meet all my monthly obligations, and in some cases I pay double." Now make a list in the first column of all your regular monthly expenses, largest to smallest. Mark them off as you pay them.

Next is the amazing part: *Take the smallest of the expenses, the last on the list, and pay it double this month.* The attainability of the small amount will help you experience the feeling of being ahead on paying bills. When you receive that bill in the mail next month, it will say, "please don't pay: you have a credit." There's no better feeling of relief and abundance than that!

Next work your way up the list, paying larger and larger bills a month ahead of time. Recite the affirmation at the top of the page, "I meet all my monthly obligations, and in some cases I pay double." Now when you get your electric bill or gas bill or phone bill, it says "please don't pay." This is the universe showering a gift upon you. Go ahead and send them money anyway just out of the appreciation of the great service they have given you, like heat, light, hot showers, or phone service. You will create a wonderful cycle of them saying "don't pay," and you sending money anyway. It feels like a gift going both directions. By just getting ahead of your bills by one month, you will create a rewarding bill experience.

This shifts the whole energy of paying bills. You will feel great about getting bills in the mail, because they will now feel like good news, and like a gift. And it all starts simply by paying ahead on one affordable bill!

I learned this technique from Abraham-Hicks. I used it starting in May of 2007, when I could barely keep up with my bills and hated them and the negative energy that they constantly brought to my mailbox. I decided to give this idea a try despite my tight financial situation, trusting that shifting my thinking, although frightening at first, would lead to more abundance and that I would be provided for. As I began to practice this method, I had more fun paying ahead on more bills, and by December I had my largest bill (my rent) paid three months in advance!

As I hope that my experience and teaching is of benefit and guidance for your life, I am honored to pass on the material for the teachers who helped form my thought journey. Explore the website www.abraham-hicks.com. I suggest that you buy one of their live workshop CDs, preferably the most recent one. There is an endless supply of wisdom in each of their discs, and it can really help you continue to find joy though the changes of your thoughts

It's not how much money you have, it's how you feel about the money you DO have.

Exercise for Paying Bills Double & Reducing Debt (Mental Money Trick)

List of Expenses from biggest to smallest:

_____

_____

_____

_____

_____

Pay the smallest one double this month and write and recite the following affirmation: "I meet all my monthly obligations, and in some cases I pay double."

As we live a life of ease, every one of us has all we need.
— The Beatles, "Yellow Submarine"

Inspired Personal Stories: Day 36

Hi Dr. Rick,

I recently had an epiphany. I have always worried about how the bills are going to get paid next month. I always had trouble seeing the answer if I didn't already have enough money socked away to meet next month's expenses, which I usually don't.

Well, one day it occurred to me that all these bills do somehow get paid. I was explaining to a friend that there always seems to be enough money in my account to cover the bills. I was stunned. I had just spoken a great and wise truth. "There is always enough money to pay the bills that come in." It's like magic. I could always see this magic in other areas of my life, but had not yet seen it in the financial arena.

Why was I worrying about something that really never happens? Why worry about where the money is going to come from to pay next month's bills, when it clearly always shows up?

So, there you go, an epiphany, many years in the making. My new affirmation: There is always enough. There is always enough. And you know what? I can really feel the emotion and the knowing of this when I recite it! And I shall work every day to hold that emotion.

— *Christopher, West Allis, Wisconsin*

Hi! Rick,

In my heart, I believe that the more you give away, the more you'll be provided with. But I still can't surrender to it. I'm still walking the tightrope when it comes to money and would like to get past that point. I'm getting too old for this! This is a new way of looking at money and will definitely change my feeling towards it! I intend to practice doubling the payment of my smallest expense until I feel comfortable with it.

— *Johanna Lopez, Quakertown, Pennsylvania*

Dear Dr. Rick,

I wanted to share something I heard Dr. Deepak Chopra say on one of his audiotapes. He related a story about being in a board meeting for a charity that wanted to do a big project that required lots of money.

One of the board members asked, "Where is all that money going to come from?" The senior member of the board, a very wise man, simply responded with, "Wherever it is right now!"

I really love that response, and I just can't get it out of my head. I keep using it in conversation all the time ... and I think it's working. More money is finding me, too! From where? Ha, from wherever it was!
— *George M., Waukesha, Wisconsin*

Dear Dr. Rick,

I wanted to share a money exercise I learned from one of the Abraham-Hicks CDs. They recommended to carry a $100 bill in your pocket all the time. So I tried it. I put a $100 bill folded up in my wallet in the clear window where I see it whenever I open it to pay for anything. It really works. I walk around all day now knowing I can buy that or buy this, right now, 'cause I have the cash.

So, instead of saying I can't afford it, or it's too expensive, I say I can buy lunch for this whole group right now, or I can buy that sweater right now. I can, I can, I can. I only actually spent it once. I usually simply choose not to. But I know I can!

Wow, what a difference. I really like the feeling, and now I can work on more money issues now that I know I can think differently about a little thing, a $100 purchase.
— *Reginald, Lincoln Park, Illinois*

Hi Dr. Rick,

When I read Day 36 I realized that is exactly how it works in my life. I had some really tough times emotionally and financially four years ago going through a divorce, and I really struggled with having enough money. Since then, my faith deepened and I was drawn closer to God and started focusing on counting my blessings. I returned to giving to charity again, primarily my church, ten percent. That act started me to feel more comfortable with money again.

So here's my summary: when I gave ten percent of my net income to charity, I felt better about money and always seemed to have enough. When I stopped, I felt like I didn't have enough. When I returned to tithing, I again felt peaceful about the money I have. Looking back, I think it is possible the feeling of "having enough" dictated the amount of money flowing in to me! And the feeling of "having enough" did not come from the amount of money I had, it came from the act of giving it away. Awesome!

The last year I have started donating ten percent of my gross income to charity. What I do is every time I get an income check and enter it into my checkbook register, I immediately follow it with a ten percent check to charity. Since that is the time I feel most financially secure, it is easy, and the giving adds to that feeling.

Now I don't worry about the income side of it, because I know that I will be blessed with enough income to meet any expenses so long as I stay with the energy of giving each time. It's fun for me to have realized and reflected on all this.

— *Marc, Indianapolis, Indiana*

Don't confuse your net worth with your self-worth.
— R.S.

Day 37

Pure Potentiality:
Plan a Trip with No Plan

Congratulations!

You have reached Day 37 in the 37-Day Workshop! Today you will have the opportunity to complete your 37th Action Step. It is focused on the ideas of potentiality.

What we know as reality is limited to one concept at a time, but the openness of potentiality creates infinite possibilities. Potentiality always is greater than known reality. Not knowing is always greater than knowing. Following are some practical examples of this to give you an idea of what I am talking about: not packing your lunch creates lots of choices for lunch; not having a spouse creates infinite possibilities of bringing in a wonderful person to marry; or not having a job creates endless career possibilities.

Now don't worry, I am not going to ask you to quit your job. The exercise today is really simple, and really effective: plan a trip with *no plan!* Sit down and schedule a vacation with a precise departure time and a precise return time. Provide no other details to the plan, except perhaps the airline flight or the initial direction your car will travel when you leave home.

Let every other detail present itself along the way.

Have you ever noticed that when you make a wrong turn, sometimes you discover something wonderful? It might be something you know you were meant to see, but you would have missed if you had stayed on track and hadn't made the wrong turn. Let this vacation be a symphony of wrong turns and unexpected surprises.

You can make it a day, or even an hour. Stop in an unexpected place and go for a walk in an area you have never walked before. See what appears for you. Whatever time period you have to dedicate to this exercise, it will help you begin to let go of your dependency on the known, the planned, the defined. Enjoy the unknown. Embrace the pure potentiality of the trip!

Surrender, and live in joy!

Let your life be a symphony of wrong turns.
— R.S.

Inspired Personal Stories: Day 37

Hi Rick,

I want to share my "surrender" life experience with you.

On the day that my journey began, I felt questions and anticipation flooding my mind: where the heck was I going and where would I end up? How long was I going to be gone? What was I going to learn and what was I going to do in London?

Unlike many people who travel to new destinations, I had not read even one travel book or even looked at a map of London. This journey was a trust walk and I wasn't going to make any plans. I trusted that I would be guided and led on the path of my highest good.

When the pilot announced that we would be landing at Heathrow in thirty minutes, I found myself wishing that someone would be waiting for me. I decided to create exactly the situation I wanted. In those few moments before touching down in a foreign country, I began to think about exactly what I believed I deserved. How could I make my first minutes in London a perfect experience?

I envisioned the exact experience that I would like to have waiting for me when I arrived. I would like a warm, nurturing person to greet me warmly with a hug, someone to help me find a place to stay and make me feel comfortable and taken care of. I would like to be welcomed into this new country and have magic happen.

As luck would have it, one of my seatmates was a man named Thomas, who was traveling to England to visit his godparents, Tom and Margaret, and explore the country a bit. When we landed, Thomas and I chatted as we stood in line waiting to go through customs; and happily found our bags at the same time.

As we passed through the final doors, a tall, gray-haired man immediately embraced Thomas. Standing next to him, practically quivering with eagerness to hug him, was a wonderful, sixtyish, warm dumpling of a woman. She asked me if I knew Thomas, to which I responded that we had sat next to each other on the plane. That was enough for her; she grabbed me and hugged me as if she were a beloved aunt whom I had not seen in years. (Well, that was just what I had asked for, much to my delight!) After embracing Thomas, the tall gentleman turned around and hugged me as well. Oh my gosh ... double hugs! What a magical manifestation.

Within moments, my new friends were whisking me off to their home to nourish me, let me rest, and help me find my new accommodations. All of my intentions were delivered, and in the most wonderful way possible!

For me, surrendering to the possibilities in the unknown is the only way to go! It was demonstrated to me that the universe can imagine it much better than I can!

— *Sunni Boehme, Life Coach, Bay View, Wisconsin*

Hello Rick,

I agree with you, believe in, and practice your affirmation, "In my world, nothing ever goes wrong." It is very much a part of surrender. I have also learned to take action from surrender, rather than passively surrender. So, I will leave you with my affirmation: "Each new unexpected outcome or 'surprise' is an opportunity." Many thanks.

— *Annie Duane, Worthington, Ohio*

Day 38
(Bonus Day)

Personal Resuscitation:
Create a Mechanism to Move from
Discouragement to Hopefulness

This Action Step is one of the key elements that is missing from nearly all the Law of Attraction resources out there. This is the answer to the most important question of all, *"What do I do when I am discouraged and I can't easily reach my optimistic positive thoughts and be able to follow the recommended action steps in this book?"*

The answer is to create a mechanism that works for you. It is different for everyone. For me it is as follows (an account from May, 2010):

"I had just returned from Florida where my oldest daughter Kate (22) and I were disposing of all of my Dad's personal possessions in his Florida winter home, as he will not be returning (he wants to stay in Milwaukee year round and be closer to family.) During the four days we were there, we literally handled and sorted every item in the house and directed it toward the antique shop, the non-profit thrift stores, or the dumpster. And he was a packrat, never letting go of any item that might have some use to someone in the future, including 25 yardsticks, and thousands of screws, nails, rusted tools, etc ... are you kidding? Well anyway, by the time we were done the home looked like a perfect furnished rental or sellable home with no visible signs of the personality that wintered there for the last 26 years.

"Here was my challenge: I consider myself non-material at this point in my life, and have spent a lot of time, energy and focus on evolving and expanding into a being that desires few, if any personal possessions. Immersing myself in sorting and handling so many possessions shifted my energy so far that I could no longer feel the "reality" of the dream world that I am used to now living in ... the world of creating, of the possible, the unknown. Now, this is my path, and my baseline. I am not suggesting that you need to be like me in any way, I just use it as an illustration of someone being true to their own desires.

"So, at this point I clearly needed my mechanism for personal resuscitation, to bring me back to the hopeful, light, positive place I like to be. I started by turning on my positive audios and letting them play continuously. I couldn't hear much at first, but just continued to let them play. Gradually, I could hear more and more in the messages. After two or three days, I could fully feel the inspiring words and feelings and I had my vibration and energy back to where I am again comfortable."

It is a great lesson and a great reminder to always have available a path back to expansion, the path that uniquely works for you. Whenever you are discouraged, it is key to know what to do, to have a mechanism, a path, an action plan to return to your uplifted state. It was wonderful to know that I could easily get back (in a few days) to my expanded state, but "wow," what a journey to take last week. Oh, and p.s., thank you thank you thank you for the incredible gift of having my daughter with me to escort me safely through what most people call the "real world." She was spectacular, and I don't know if I'd have been able to do it without her!

Each time I find myself flat on my face, I pick myself up and get back in the race ... That's Life!
— Dean Kay and Kelly Gordon

Additional reading about the obstacles that can prevent us from experiencing the joy that is possible in this life.

If you would like to read a report on the obstacles that stand in the way of us mastering positive thinking and getting the Law of Attraction working for us the way we want, go to www.rickschaefermd.com and click on "It's Not Your Fault: the Nine Reasons Report."

You will find nine specific, natural (learned) behaviors that you may be completely unaware of that are blocking you. This will allow you to understand what needs to be shifted in order to truly get these techniques to work for you.

Personal Examples of Resuscitation Mechanisms

I wanted to collect a few real life examples of what people who understand this step do to consciously move from discouragement to hopefulness. There is great diversity in this list, but the important thing is finding out what works for YOU, and knowing your personal mechanism. Oh yeah, and then remembering to use it!
— R.S.

I'll do two things. First is to connect with good friends (only two or three) who truly know me and can be there as a support. Secondly I will do something physical to help energize myself while listening to upbeat music. In summer it's easy; walking, biking, golfing, shooting hoops, etc. In winter it might be just doing some exercises at home, but walking on a crisp winter day is great, too. The key is the positive music while getting the heart pumping. Reading life affirmations or the Psalms is also in the mix. Works every time.
— Chris Wacker

I pull out my oils and brushes. Working on a painting puts me in my right brain. Time loses all importance and my mind is so engaged that there is no allowance of negative thoughts.
— Dr. Gael Riverz

When I need hope and inspiration I always pick up *The Power of Your Subconscious Mind* by Joseph Murphy and read a page or chapter.

It was the first book I ever read in 1975 that started my

spiritual awakening and it continues to inspire me and kick my butt.
— *Sunni Boehme*

I do one of two things. I take a deep breath and ask myself what would my Grandpa do in this situation or what advice would he give me, and it puts a smile on my face and me back on track. Or, I stop, look around, and remind myself how blessed I am with amazing friends and family and "stuff" that quickly reminds me that I have all the hope in the world.
— *Kevin Kowalke*

Yes ... this is an easy one for me. No matter what the problem ... personal, business, whatever; I simply throw one hundred percent of myself into something that keeps me busy such as a remodeling project, cleaning the basement or garage, or organizing something that I have been putting off. Mostly I just throw myself into my work. Usually, if it is something I want to forget, I do the mindless stuff. If it is something I want to improve in my life, I choose the work. Either way, it feels great to accomplish more and gets me back on track.
— *Bill Driscoll*

To share what I do when I am truly discouraged, I need to share a story. As a young Marine in boot camp long ago, I was on a painful, twenty-mile march in one hundred degree heat and choking dust through the dry hills of Camp Pendleton. I suffered a blinding headache, and my body hurt from fatigue as the straps of my backpacks pressed deep into sore muscles. We were only half way there, and I was about to break down—no way could I last another ten miles.

My sergeant read my face and yelled, "When you think

you're going under, don't think about what's far off. If you think about the whole thing, you'll get overwhelmed and give up. Just focus on the next step, the next step ..."

I did, and it worked. I have used this wisdom during other hardships in my life. I bear down and focus on the next step, the next task, the next customer, or the next hour and avoid thinking of the awful big picture. Focus on the next step. Better times will come later. And they have, every single time.
— *Al Guyant*

I cry—out loud and *really hard*—and whine in a mirror until I get angry enough to act. "If, at first, I don't succeed, I try, try again."
— *Johanna Lopez*

When I am drowning and need a life preserver, I literally stop myself, grab my unconditional love buddies (my dogs), and take a long walking meditation, focusing on breathing in and breathing out, aware of being alive. There is nothing like connecting with my source, my Buddha self, to bring me back to a place of hope and joy.
— *Teri Williams*

When I am discouraged, I let myself feel the fullness of the feeling, understand what it is, and then find a softer thought about it. Some hopeful thought. Then I let that feeling build, and listen to an audio recording that fits my mood and that will bring me up higher from there. Then repeat, and repeat.
— *Judy Corkle*

I know when I need to revert to my "mechanism"—when I feel out of balance, nervous, and have a "stomach ache." I call it "stop, drop and roll." First I feel it for a while, then I take very deep breaths, drink a huge glass of water, and then think of one thing to be in gratitude of: perhaps my coffee, running water for a shower, some small item. Feeling a tiny bit better, I then plan something fun for me: a concert, dancing, a run around the neighborhood. For me, it is always something with a change of scenery, so I can see life from a new vantage point.

— *Judy Sandvick*

~~End Note~~

... the Beginning!

Congratulations! By completing this program, you have created your own path to Maximum Life! I hope you now understand that everything you need is already inside you. You are continually connected to the infinite intelligence and wisdom of the universe, and you can access divine intervention at all times. Remember, everything is an "inside" job!

I truly hope that you enjoyed reading this book as much as I enjoyed writing it. You have now worked all the way through your Extreme Thought Makeover™. Now the challenge before you is to keep it going; to never, ever, ever stop! Let's discuss some ways to keep the transformation going with the resources that follow.

Moving forward, I'd first like you to reflect on what you have done, what you have accomplished, and the feeling of it all as you accomplished it. The next chapter is designed for that reflection. Please take time to do it. I suggest returning to reflect on a weekly basis. Also, you may consider reflecting on a random chapter anytime. It's amazing how the right answer will appear from a "random" peek when you feel you need a little something.

Next follows the Workbook Chapter. This contains a list of ongoing steps from ten selected lessons that act as a guide each day to insure that you continue to expand upon what you have done, and don't fall back into old habits. Launch into continual growing and expanding by following the Daily Ongoing Steps. This form is the actual copy that I use on a daily (or nearly daily) basis.

One of these steps is the daily feeding of your heart with an inspirational audio (Day 3). This will guarantee your continuing expansion, because each day you will hear something that can inspire you to keep going.

Keep your Personal Resuscitation Mechanism from the preceding chapter with you at all times, so that you always have a pathway back to joy whenever discouragement creeps in. Then keep going and going. You will find more and more. And everything you find can potentially have a greater and greater effect than anything that came before. Open yourself up to it. Let it all in.

This is about joy, always reaching for more joy. There is always more and more and more. You will never be done. It is the process, and feeling the hope, embracing the ultimate knowing that it can and will get better and better and better. And, the better is gets, the better it gets!

There is always more!

With love,
Rick

Reflection:
Summary of the 37 Lessons

Let's reflect on what you have experienced over the course of this book. Let's review each of the lessons and try to re-capture the feeling of being immersed in it again for the first time. Many lessons will have simple feelings associated with them, just happy uplifting thoughts. Some lessons will have very strong positive experiences and gratefulness linked to them. I suggest you particularly focus right now on the lessons that really brought something to you at the time. Reflect on the feeling it brings up now.

I suggest you sit comfortably, and put on some soothing relaxing music. It can heighten your ability to capture and recapture those feelings. Enjoy ...

Where you are is just fine.

Day 0 Healing Energy: We simply found videos and audios that made us laugh.

Day 1 Good Stuff: We placed items with positive meanings for us in plain sight around our home and office.

Day 2 Appreciation: We created a written list of things we are appreciative of, and we went on and on in a "rampage" or "avalanche." Try this one every day for a week and see what happens!

Day 3 A Lifetime of Learning: We made a commitment to listen to something uplifting in the morning during our bathroom grooming time. We found audio-books with very positive messages for us.

Day 4 Productivity: We created a list of the five most significant things we wanted to get done the following day, and then worked on them first thing in the morning ... first #1, then #2.

Day 5 Appreciating Others: We made a commitment to send one card of appreciation every day, ideally an unexpected card.

Day 6 Self-Love: We found a picture from our childhood and imagined what we wish for that beautiful and perfect child.

Day 7 Finding New Love: We created a list of attributes we like about ourselves. We learned the most powerful way to attract the perfect lover.

Day 8 Charity: We committed to give something away every day ... a hug, a $5 tip, etc.

Day 9 Affirmations: We wrote messages and affirmations very meaningful to us, and with specific appreciation to members of our families, and posted them conspicuously around our home and/or office.

Day 10 Detachment: We made a commitment to throw something away everyday to decrease our physical clutter and thus our mental clutter.

Day 11 Anonymous Charity: We bought a meal for another without recognition to embrace the feeling privately.

Day 12 Productivity II: We committed to control who we speak with and when by scheduling phone and email contact according to *our* own preference.

Day 13 Self-Love II : We created a list of all we like about our bodies ... chemical, physical, electrical, mechanical ... and expanded and expanded it.

Day 14 Wealth Consciousness: We sent ourselves a check just for the feeling of receiving great big checks in the mailbox.

Day 15 Consistency of Thought: We learned how to avoid confrontation and judgment around our ideals, and to insulate ourselves from negative opinions and criticism from others.

Day 16 Owning Your Thought Sphere: We practiced keeping out unwanted negative energy and thought programming by avoiding the TV news, TV commercials, and radio or newspapers.

Day 17 Humanism Over Nationalism: We simply bought a coffee mug with a global positive message to reinforce our perspective of all of humanity being of one energy of love and desire.

Day 18 Possibilities: We gave away our last $5 when our wallet was nearly empty and embraced the potential of the Universe filling the void.

Day 19 Triggering Positive Energy Unexpectedly: We reprogrammed our ring-tones on our cell-phones to be positive uplifting melodies for us.

Day 20 Manifestation: We created a Dream Board or "Genie Board" and posted pictures of what we wanted to bring into our lives in order to focus our attention on those items and concepts.

Day 21 Focus of Thought: We sat in silence for five minutes and tried to quiet our minds to concentrating on only one thing at a time.

Day 22 Parenting With Love: We displayed a picture of our children at a young, super lovable age in our wallets so that we would be reminded daily with the image of how madly in love with us they are.

Day 23 Imagination: We created an imaginative story of what the perfect day for us would be like. Thus, we allow it all to happen by writing about it and thinking about it.

Day 24 Openness and Learning: We created a new habit of listening to audio-books in our car as we drive to aid in our learning, increase our openness to ideas, and to bring peace to our drive time.

Day 25 Self-Love III: We experimented with the idea of consistently putting ourselves first in order to be filled with love, enough to be able to endlessly shower that love on others.

Day 26 Your Contact Sphere: We privately created an up-lifters list and evaluated who represented the greatest positive influence in our lives, and who might represent an emotional drain to us.

Day 27 Love of Humanity: We practiced using words of love that we would like to hear from others. We practiced using them with people that we may not totally agree with, and that represent a personal emotional challenge to us.

Day 28 Exercise and Fitness: We created a habit of using an exercise list daily with very modest goals that we could meet and exceed every day in order to create an affirmation of accomplishment around our exercise goals.

Day 29 Finding the Perfect Career: We created a life mission statement, clumsy at first, and refined it many times in order to clearly guide us toward our ideal career, one that matches our purpose in life and can be truly satisfying.

Day 30 Mental Programming: We went though our music collection and transformed what we listen to up to a higher vibration so that the programming coming from the music would be feeding us and expanding us spiritually and emotionally.

Day 31 Diet, Nutrition, and Weight Loss: We worked on some affirmation exercises to remove the fear around the food we eat, and learn to trust the natural cravings of our bodies.

Day 32 Alleviating Worry and Living in the Now: We used the simple action of taking a walk to focus our consciousness completely in the present tense, thus decreasing regret and resentment from the past, and decreasing worry around the future.

Day 33 Restoring Your Health: We explored the infinite intelligence that lives in each cell in our bodies. We considered the connected energy that ties all the billions of these cells together perfectly by mechanical, chemical, and electrical means. Based on this energetic perfection within us, we learned that disease is simply our own resisting and obstructing the natural, healthy state that desires to manifest at all times.

Day 34 Endless Possibilities: We hung a new blank canvas on our wall as an exercise in seeing what we desire in the picture, in our relationships, and in our lives.

Day 35 Embracing Diversity: We explored the power and majesty of the perfection of each of the seven billion of us on this planet perceiving everything a little differently, and having a different perspective. We practiced allowing and accepting those perspectives, and giving up the desire to have others agree with us.

Day 36 Wealth Consciousness II: We worked an exercise to help us accept mentally that we always have enough money, and that we can indeed meet all our financial obligations, and often exceed them.

Day 37 Pure Potentiality: We simply planned a trip with no plan to discover how much more of the world and the Universe we can let in when we do not try to control it or prejudge it. We found that this relates to relationships, health, career, finances, parenting ... well, every aspect of our lives.

Day 38 Personal Resuscitation: We created a mechanism personally for us that works to help us when we feel discouraged. We created an action step to help us move at any time from discouragement to hopefulness.

Reflections: Oh, we reflected upon all the wonderful emotional expansion we underwent during our journey through this book and the 37 Day Program. We then committed to an ongoing set of daily action steps to keep the expansion in place, and growing. We committed to honor these expanded and uplifted emotions by reviewing this Reflection List on a regular basis. Wow, we really did have an Extreme Thought Makeover™. Woo-Hoo!!! Let's do it again!

And in the end, the love you take is equal to the love you make.
— The Beatles, "The End"

Workbook:
Ongoing Activities After the 37 Days

There are ten Lessons that have ongoing activity recommendations, requiring 18 to 28 minutes of your time per day. By keeping up with this, you will ensure your path to Maximum Life. Here's a review:

- Listen to an audio book while grooming
- Send one unexpected card of appreciation
- Write one positive personal attribute
- Choose one body part to adore
- Write your Five Things List
- Toss something out
- Sit in silence for five minutes
- Take a five-minute walk outside
- Give a gift (give a hug or a $5 tip)
- Daily Exercise List

The time it takes to accomplish all of this might be as much as 28 minutes, which is actually less than the time it used to take you to read the newspaper or watch one TV news show.

On days you really feel like writing, add the Weekly Activities List. This includes re-writing a few of your favorite affirmations, re-writing your Life Mission Statement, re-writing your Personal Resuscitation Mechanism, and going on a written Rampage of Appreciation. Whenever you are making a major decision in your life about how you spend your time or a commitment to a job or career choice, bring yourself back to your Life Mission Statement. Test the decision choices against your Statement, and see how they match up with your life mission.

The following two forms will help you. I suggest you fill out the first one, the Daily Activities List, every day. Fill in the 5 Things List portion before you go to sleep, and it will be working for you as you are sleeping. You will wake up with the drive and focus to address the first two things on the list immediately. As an example, that is exactly how this chapter got written: "Last evening I set the intention to write the on-going Daily Activities List into this book. When I awoke this morning, 5:55 a.m. June 20th, 2010, Father's Day, I was ready to immediately go to my laptop and do this writing."

It is amazing how much focus and drive and set intention can come from a night of sleep after going to bed knowing what the one or two most significant tasks are that you want to accomplish the next day.

Please use these forms daily. Keep them with you throughout the day, and celebrate all the Daily Activities you have completed as the day goes on. Use these forms over and over and over. And whenever you find yourself falling out of the habit of using them ... start using them again. It works!

Note: You can find downloadable files of these forms on my website at www.rickschaefermd.com under the link "Book Resources."

Extreme Thought Makeover™ Daily Activities List

Complete these ten tasks daily to ensure the continuing expansion of your Extreme Thought Makeover™:

1. Write your 5 Things List (Day 4), and do the top two:

    1) _____

    2) _____

    3) _____

    4) _____

    5) _____

2. Audio Education (Day 3) in the bathroom and/or car. Choose a recording:

_____

3. Write one positive personal attribute (Day 7):

_____

4. Choose one body part to admire (Day 13):

_____

5. Send an unexpected card of appreciation (Day 5). Choose a recipient:

_____

6. Take a walk for five minutes (Day 32): ____

7. Sit in silence for five minutes (Day 21): ____

8. Give a gift or a $5 tip (Day 8): ____

9. Toss something out to un-clutter your physical space and thus your mental space (Day 10): ____

10. Exercise list (Day 28):

_____ 1 sit-up   ____ 1 push-up   ____ 1 pull-up

_____ 1 squat   ____ 1 stretch   ____ 1 breath

Extreme Thought Makeover™ Suggested Weekly Writing Assignment

Write some personal affirmations (how you desire your life to be today, from Day 9, 25, and really every other day in the program):

_____

_____

_____

Rewrite your life mission statement (Day 29):

_____

_____

_____

Write your Personal Resuscitation Mechanism (Day 38):

_____

_____

_____

Go on a Rampage of Appreciation (Day 2):

_____

_____

_____

Okay, you're going to need some more paper for this one!

Recommended Reading and Resources

Recommended Reading

Arntz, William, Betsy Chase, and Mark Vicente. *What the Bleep Do We Know,* 2007.

Bateman, Kody. *Promptings, Your Inner Guide to Making a Difference,* 2009, (Day 5).

Bryne, Rhonda. *The Secret,* 2006, (Days 20, 29).

Buscaglia, Leo. *Love,* 1972.

Canfield, Jack and Hansen, Mark Victor. *A 4ᵗʰ Course of Chicken Soup for the Soul,* 1997, "You Don't Bring Me Flowers Anymore," (Day 5).

Chopra, Deepak, M.D. *The Seven Spiritual Laws of Success,* 1994, (Days 33, 37).

Dallman-Jones, Anthony, Ph.D. *Primary Domino Thinking,* 1997, (Foreword).

Dispenza, Dr. Joe. *Evolve Your Brain: The Science of Changing Your Mind,* 2008, (Day 33).

Dyer, Dr. Wayne W. *There Is a Spiritual Solution to Every Problem,* 2002.

Ecker, T. Harv. *Secrets of the Millionaire Mind, Mastering the Inner Game of Wealth,* 2005.

Emoto, Dr. Masaru. *The True Power of Water: Healing and Discovering Ourselves,* 2005, (Day 33).

Ferriss, Timothy. *The 4-Hour Workweek,* 2007, (Day 12).

Fulghum, Robert. *All I Really Need To Know I Learned in Kindergarten,* 2004.

Hawkins, Dr. David. *Truth vs. Falsehood,* 2005, page 97 for the Energy of Music Scale, (Day 30).

Hay, Louise. *You Can Heal Your Life,* 1984, (Day 33).

Hicks, Jerry and Esther. *Ask and It Is Given,* 2005, (Days 2, 36).

Hill, Napoleon. *Think and Grow Rich!: The Original Version, Restored and Revised,* 2004, (Day 3).

Siegel, Bernie, M.D. *Love, Medicine and Miracles: Lessons Learned about Self-Healing from a Surgeon's Experience with Exceptional Patients,* 1990, (Day 33).

Tolle, Eckhart. *The Power of Now,* 2004, (Day 32).

Winninger, Toni Ann, and Peter Watson Jenkins. *Talking With Leaders of the Past,* 2008.

Recommended Resources

Dumb & Dumber, Saturday Night Live, America's Funniest Home Videos (Day 0).

Nightingale, Earl. *The Strangest Secret,* audio CD, remastered 2000, (Day 4).

Nightingale, Earl. "The $25,000 Idea," story found online (Day 4).

Teachings of Abraham Workshops audio recordings by Jerry and Esther Hicks (Day 2), www.abraham-hicks.com.

SendOutCards: www.sendoutcards.com; see also video tour link at www.rickschaefermd.com (Day 5).

"It's Not Your Fault: 9 Reasons Report" by Rick Schaefer, M.D. Found at www.rickschaefermd.com, (Day 38).

These resources can be found at www.rickschaefermd.com. Direct links are provided on the site to the books, audios, MP3s, etc. to help you connect to the exact edition referenced in the 37 Day Program and on this list.

If you'd like to share your own Inspired Personal Stories with Dr. Rick, please email them to rickschaefermd@me.com. Dr. Rick will post many of them on his blog and testimonial pages. Also, you might wind up in the next book!

And please feel free to add comments to Dr. Rick's Blog at www.rickschaefermd.com/blog. These comments will likely be very valuable to other readers across the globe.

More from Dr. Rick and Extreme Thought Makeover™

Dr. Rick has a private, personalized ten-week coaching program that includes daily emails, weekly one-on-one phone sessions, and about fifteen minutes of homework every other day.

He is also available for private phone consultation.

His appearance schedule and other recommended resources including forms for download, audios, videos, articles, blogs, and of course mugs, are available through his website http://www.rickschaefermd.com

You will also find a plethora of free articles and blogs there, and opportunities to interact with him by leaving testimonials and comments.

Rick Schaefer, M.D.
Extreme Thought Makeover™, LLC

Mailing Address:
P.O. Box 5333
Elm Grove, WI 53122
414-573-8880
http://www.rickschaefermd.com

"Give Me 18-28 Minutes a Day for 37 Days, and this Fun and Simple Program Will Transform Your Life!"

CPSIA information can be obtained at www.ICGtesting.com
Printed in the USA
LVOW07*0210120713

342332LV00001B/1/P

9 780984 388301